JUSTICE OR REVOLUTION

America's Choice in the 1980's

BY

LESLIE SNYDER

BOOKS IN FOCUS Inc.
bringing you books that matter

Other Books By Leslie Snyder

Why Gold?
Gold and Black Gold

Manufactured in the United States of America

Library of Congress Catalog Card Number 78-74594

ISBN 0-916728-20-x

Books In Focus, Inc.
Suite 31B
160 East 38th Street
New York, N.Y. 10016

Telephone: (212) 490-0334

CONTENTS

To George Conway

Preface

The purpose of this book is to prove that justice, which is the cornerstone of this nation, is disappearing; and that without justice, this nation, as we know it, shall perish.

Daniel Webster said, "Justice is the great interest of man on earth." Perhaps when he said that in 1845 it was true. But today few people are concerned about justice; hence we have a multitude of problems—both individual, national, and international. The solutions to these problems—dishonesty, lack of integrity, currency depreciation (inflation), oppressive government, rebellions, wars, etc.—lie in the study and practice of justice.

According to the great American constitutional lawyer of the nineteenth century, Lysander Spooner, justice is "The science of mine and thine—the science of justice—is the science of all human rights; of all a man's rights of person and property; of all his rights to life, liberty, and the pursuit of happiness."

Therefore, justice encompasses all things relating to life. And the vulgar, indiscriminate injustices we are witnessing today are a result of mischievous and ill-advised political action. The theme of this book is the study of politics and how to re-establish justice. For when injustice invades the political sphere, rebellion ensues. The difference between rebellion and revolution is that a rebellion is a violent, desperate social action of a few, whereas revolution is a thought-out, principled political action undertaken by the majority. Yes, a rebellion is in the making; and it could overturn all the achievements of the American Revolution. Consequently, it becomes clear why a thorough study of justice is now imperative. Re-establishing justice is the *only* way to regain and insure our liberties and to prevent a violent rebellion in the not too distant future.

Today few people actively believe in the importance of justice. But just as justice promotes peace and harmony in society, so injustices and tyrannies foment unrest and rebellion. It is either/or. They are simply two sides of the same coin.

Our government has no money of its own; it is not independently wealthy. It is dependent on taxes and the issue of legal tender for all its income and funds. The current re-distribution of wealth being conducted by government in the name of social equality is, in reality, a distribution of injustices. This government action of force over individual initiative, of coercion over freedom, can end only one way. As wealth is surely being destroyed, so is justice. And, while tyranny emerges, the American genius and spirit submerges. All forms of freedom and property are thereby perishing.

The following words were written to describe Britain's designs on the American colonies:

> If I told you that a deep-laid and desperate plan of imperial despotism has been laid, and partly executed, for the extinction of all civil liberties, would you believe it? If I told you that a corrupt and prostituted government is pointing its destructive machines against the sacred liberties of Americans, attempting by every device to enslave the people and plunder them of their property and, what is more, their birthright, liberty, would you believe it?

Few people ever see the logical and inevitable consequences of specific actions. But there is a definite relationship between cause and effect. The cause is injustice; the effect is revolution. The colonists believed their lives and liberties were in jeopardy. They went to war to throw off the despots and to establish a new and free government. We need not go that far—yet. We still have redress to our government, in order that justice and our rights be re-established once again. But we must act soon!

Revolution is in the air today. This book, by pointing out the consequences of gross injustices, hopes to stave off a violent rebellion.

Do you see a revolution in the making? On January 29, 1848, the great French philosopher, Alexis de Tocqueville, stood up in the French Chamber of Deputies to warn his fellow politicians of another revolution under way:

> I am told that there is no danger because there are no riots; I am told that, because there is no visible disorder on the surface of society, there is no revolution at hand.
>
> Gentlemen, permit me to say that I believe you are mistaken. True, there is no actual disorder, but it has

> entered deeply into men's minds....can you not see that their passions, instead of political, have become social? Do you not see that they are gradually forming opinions and ideas that destine not only to upset this or that law, ministry, or even form of government, but society itself, until it totters upon the foundations on which it rests today? Do you not listen to what they say to themselves each day? Do you not hear them repeating unceasingly that all that is above them is incapable and unworthy of governing them; that the distribution of goods prevalent until now throughout the world is unjust; that property rests on a foundation that is not an equitable one? And do you not realize that when such opinions take root, when they are spread in almost a universal manner, when they sink deeply into the masses, they are bound to bring with them sooner or later, I know not when or how, a most formidable revolution?
>
> I believe that we are at this moment sleeping on a volcano....
>
> When I come to investigate what...has brought about the downfall of the governing classes, I perceive...the effective reason that causes men to lose political power is that they have become unworthy to retain it.
>
> ...the governing class had become, through its indifference, its selfishness, and its vices, incapable and unworthy of governing the country.
>
> I speak here without bitterness; I am even addressing you without any party spirit; I am attacking men against whom I feel no vindictiveness. But I am obliged to communicate my firm and profound conviction...that public morality is being degraded, and that the degradation of public morality will shortly, very shortly perhaps, bring down upon you new revolutions....
>
> Yes, the danger is great. Allay it while there is yet time; correct the evil by efficacious remedies, by attacking it not in its symptoms, but in itself.
>
> Legislative changes have been spoken of. I am greatly disposed to think that these changes are not only very useful, but necessary....But, in God's name, change the spirit of the government; for, I repeat, that spirit will lead you to the abyss."[1]

After the speech, de Tocqueville observed that the politicians had lost all ability to perceive reality; they did not believe him. One month later Louis Philippe's bourgeois monarchy of nearly twenty years fell

[1] *A Treasury of the World's Great Speeches,* Selected and edited by Houston Peterson, Grolier Inc., New York, 1973, Pp. 454-58.

like a ripe, or rather, a rotten apple. The ensuing revolution was finally settled by the rifles and cannon of General Cavaignac, paving the way for Louis Napoleon and the second French Republic.

This book is about eternal principles—specifically liberty, property, and justice. Their understanding should make today's problems knowable and solvable. Liberty, property, and independence are preserved by defending justice. But to ignore justice, to seek security by appeasement and abasement, is to lose liberty, independence, prosperity, and security forever.

The first thirteen chapters of this book investigate, examine and analyze the principles of good and evil, in just and unjust societies, as they pertain to both politics and economics. They lay the groundwork, the foundation of all *legitimate* governments. The next six chapters explore the most obvious and destructive evils that exist in the United States today. If these evils were removed, as justice demands, then tyranny would disappear and justice would be re-established.

Today, Americans are being polarized. We are being set against each other: Democrat *vs.* Republican, liberal *vs.* conservative, rich *vs.* poor, black *vs.* white, government employees *vs.* private sector, big business and banks *vs.* consumers, and on and on it goes. While we are fighting among ourselves, the enemy grows stronger. We are being divided and thus conquered. What is the enemy? It is the spirit with which we live our lives and run the country. It is an idea—a word. The enemy is *injustice*, i.e., *tyranny*. Once started, the injustices multiply, perpetuate each other, and develop into a social system until there is no justice remaining.

It is said that half the solution to a problem lies in defining it. This book not only defines the problem, but offers solutions. And it does so by using the examples and lessons of history, for there is little, if anything, that has not been done, tried, suffered, or endured before us. And those who do not learn from history tend to relive it.

The matter of justice must be everyone's concern. It is an essential part of life in society. This is *OUR* country—not yours, not mine, not some lobbyists—IT IS *OURS!* We have the right to enjoy it and the responsibility to protect and defend it. Young and old, rich and poor, all of us must wish to see justice done to each individual equally. Therefore, part of the purpose of this book is to try to re-unite opposing factions, to instill a reverence for justice. Americans must want to see justice for all; otherwise, there is justice for none. This great country, built on the glorious principles of liberty and justice for all, must reaffirm its ideals; we have but to will it. The alternative is tyranny, unrest, and the disintegration of our beloved country. Time is running out, however. All honest individuals should be able to agree on the essence and importance of justice.

Battle Ground, Washington **Leslie Snyder**
October 17, 1978

I

Justice

The administration of a republic is supposed to be directed by certain fundamental principles of right and justice, from which there cannot, because there ought not to, be any deviation; and whenever any deviation appears, there is a kind of stepping out of the republican principle, and an approach toward the despotic one.

THOMAS PAINE

The purpose of this book is to instill in the reader an understanding for the nobility of and a love for the administration of justice, because justice is the only foundation upon which a society of free and independent people can exist. Justice is a concrete, recognizable, and objective principle. It is not a matter of opinion. Hence, this chapter will define precisely what justice is.

In our day and age the word justice is rarely used in political and economic discussions. The entire reason for the existence of communities, laws, governments and court systems has been forgotten. But if life and property are to be protected and secured, which is the purpose of society, then justice *must* be the rule. To quote Paine again, "A republic, properly understood, is a sovereignty of justice."

According to a 1931 Webster's dictionary, justice is the "quality of being just; impartiality." Just is "conforming to right; normal; equitable". A 1961 Webster's dictionary says justice is "The principle of rectitude and just dealings of men with each other—one of the cardinal virtues. Administration of law... " A 1975 edition of a Grolier Webster dictionary says justice is "Equitableness; what is rightly due; lawfulness...."

Since 1931 a new meaning of the word justice has been added, that of lawfulness, which is not only erroneous, but deceitful and misleading. Justice is not based on law; rather, law ought to be based on justice. It is only common sense, for men lived and worked together before laws were formed. Generally laws are passed to formalize what has preceded under common practice, what has stood the test of time as being just and equitable. Laws are common practice put down in black and white for all to see and know.

The ancient philosophers said that justice is speaking the truth and paying your debts, giving to each man what is proper to him, doing good to friends and evil to enemies. Therefore, there must be something more basic, more fundamental than laws on which to found justice. In fact, the French jurist Charles de Montesquieu (1689-1755) ably contended that "before laws were made, there were relations of possible justice. To say that there is nothing just or unjust but what is commanded or forbidden by positive laws, is the same as saying that before the describing of a circle all the radii were not equal."[1]

The Greek philosophers had the simplest definition of justice. To Plato (c.428 B.C.-348 B.C.), in *The Republic*, Book IV, justice is simply "doing one's own business, and not being a busybody.... A man may neither take what is another's, nor be deprived of what is his own.... This is the ultimate cause and condition of the existence of all" other virtues in the State, "and while remaining in them is also their preservative."[2]

In Book XII of Plato's *Laws,* the conclusion is drawn that "by the relaxation of that justice which is the uniting principle of all constitutions, every power in the state is rent asunder from every other."[3] In other words, without justice the threads of society unravel and society disintegrates into barbarism.

Aristotle (384-322 B.C.) in *Nicomachean Ethics*, Book V, gives greater perception to what justice is. It "is found among men who share their life with a view to self-sufficiency, men who are free.... Therefore *justice is essentially something human*." (Emphasis added) In other words, free men may choose to be just or unjust. Justice, as an ethical term, is voluntary; "...a man acts unjustly or justly whenever he does such acts voluntarily."[4] When wrong is done and done voluntarily, it then becomes an act of injustice. In short, "All virtue is summed up in dealing justly," said Aristotle.

More concretely, Aristotle claims, in *Rhetoric*, Book I, "Justice is the virtue through which everybody enjoys his own possessions in accordance with the law; its opposite is injustice, through which men enjoy the possessions of others in defiance of the law."[5] The problem of using the law to legalize theft and to redistribute the property of one group to another group will be handled fully in later chapters. For the time being, we must assume Aristotle means the use of laws that are rightful and just. For when he says "justice has been acknowledged by us to be a social virtue, and it implies all others,"[6] he has laid the foundation of a just society.

Furthermore, Aristotle maintains that "legal justice is the discrimination of the just and the unjust." And, "Of political justice part is natural, part legal—natural, that which everywhere has the same force and does not exist by people's thinking this or that."[7] Natural justice must precede law and form the basis of law thereon.

In the sixteenth century Michel de Montaigne (1533-1592), in his *The Essays*, eloquently said: "The justice which in itself is natural and universal, is otherwise and more nobly ordered, than that other justice, which is special, national, and constrained to the ends of government."[8] He continues, "There cannot a worse state of things be imagined, than where wickedness comes to be legitimate, and assumes with the magistrate's permission, the cloak of virtue.... The extremest sort of injustice, according to Plato, is where that which is unjust, should be reputed for just."[9]

In Thomas Hobbes' (1588-1679) *Leviathan*, further ground is laid on which to base natural justice. The names just and unjust, says Hobbes, when they are attributed to men's actions, signify conformity or nonconformity to reason. Therefore, "Justice...is a rule of reason by which we are forbidden to do anything destructive to our life, and consequently a law of nature."[10]

Then Hobbes leads beautifully into the virtue of just actions: "That which gives to human actions the relish of justice is a certain nobleness or gallantness of courage, rarely found, by which a man scorns to be beholding for the contentment of his life to fraud, or breach of promise. This justice of the manners is that which is meant where justice is called a *virtue*; and injustice, a *vice*."[11]

Earlier it was established that justice is the social virtue on which a just society is constructed. Hobbes adds to this not only by tying virtues to the laws of nature, but to moral philosophy as well. "Now the science of virtue and vice is moral philosophy; and therefore the true doctrine of the laws of nature is the true moral philosophy.... For moral philosophy is nothing else but the science of what is good and evil in the conversation and society of mankind." [12] Thus, Hobbes establishes the fact that a *just society is a moral society*—a key premise in this book.

Saint Augustine (354-430) in *The City of God*, Book XIX, declares "Where, therefore, there is no true justice there can be no right. For that which is done right is justly done, and what is unjustly done cannot be done by right." [13] Hence, justice precedes "rights."

Joseph Joubert eloquently phrased justice as truth in action.

Since practicing the virtue of justice is voluntary, man ought to have the courage to stand up and fight for what is right and against what is wrong. Cato the Younger said it this way: "...a man has it in his power to be just, if he have but the will to be so, and therefore injustice is thought the most dishonorable because it is least excusable." [14]

Another way to consider what justice is, is to compare it with injustice. For example, in *Utilitarianism,* John Stuart Mill (1806-1873) states that "...it is just to respect, unjust to violate, the *legal rights* of any one." Second, "...injustice consists in taking or withholding from any person that to which he has a *moral right*." Third, "It is universally considered just that each person should obtain that (whether good or evil) which he *deserves*." Fourth, "It is confessedly unjust to break faith with any one: to violate an engagement, either express or implied..." Fifth, "It is, by universal admission, inconsistent with justice to be partial." [15]

Mill, too, sees justice as a moral issue. He concludes: "Whether the injustice consists in depriving a person of a possession, or in breaking faith with him, or in treating him worse than he deserves, or worse than other people who have no greater claims, in each case the supposition implies two things—a wrong done, and some assignable person who is wronged. Injustice may also be done by treating a person better than others; but the wrong in this case is to his competitors, who are also assignable persons.... Justice implies something which it is not only right to do, and wrong not to do, but which some individual person can claim from us as his moral right." [16]

Thomas Paine's *Dissertations* speak about justice where the public good is concerned. He maintains that, "The foundation-principle of public good is justice, and wherever justice is impartially administered, the public good is promoted; for as it is to the good of every man that no injustice be done to him, so likewise it is to his good that the principle which secures him should not be violated in the person of another, because such a violation weakens *his* security, and leaves to chance what ought to be to him a rock to stand on."

The great constitutional lawyer Lysander Spooner wrote a pamphlet entitled *Natural Law, or The Science of Justice* which eloquently summarizes what justice is.This will be the standard, the guideline, for this book.

> It is the science which alone can tell any man what he can, and cannot, do; what he can, and cannot have; what he can, and cannot, say, without infringing the rights of any other person.
>
> It is the science of peace; and the only science of peace; since it is the science which alone can tell us on what conditions mankind can live in peace, or ought to live in peace, with each other.
>
> These conditions are simply these: viz., first, that each man shall do, towards every other, all that justice requires him to do; as, for example, that he shall pay his debts, that he shall return borrowed or stolen property to its owner, and that he shall make reparation for any injury he may have done to the person or property of another.
>
> The second condition is, that each man shall abstain from doing to another, anything which justice forbids him to do; as, for example, that he shall abstain from committing theft, robbery, arson, murder, or any other crime against the person or property of another.
>
> So long as these conditions are fulfilled, men are at peace, and ought to remain at peace, with each other. But when either of these conditions is violated, men are at war. And they must necessarily remain at war until justice is re-established.
>
> Through all time, so far as history informs us, wherever mankind have attempted to live in peace with each other, both the natural instincts, and the collective wisdom of the human race, have acknowledged and pre-

> scribed, as an indispensable condition, obedience to this one only universal obligation: viz., that each should live honestly towards every other.
>
> The ancient maxim makes the sum of man's legal duty to his fellow men to be simply this: "*To live honestly, to hurt no one, to give to every one his due...*"
>
> If there be in nature such a principle as justice, it is necessarily the only political principle there ever was, or ever will be. All the other so-called political principles, which men are in the habit of inventing, are not principles at all. They are either the mere conceits of simpletons, who imagine they have discovered something better than truth, and justice, and universal law; or they are mere devices and pretenses, to which selfish and knavish men resort as means to get fame, and power, and money."

Never has such a complex subject as justice been treated so clearly and simply. To summarize justice thus far: Justice means that each must be accountable for his own actions, entitled to the reward of his labor, and responsible for the consequences of his wrong doings.

The love of justice should be instilled in every man, woman and child—all should wish to see justice done. For without justice the rule of men (dictatorship), not of law, assumes power. Without justice there is no security for life, liberty, and property. Without justice, society disintegrates into barbarism, where courts of law are administered by favor and pull instead of objective law, and without objective laws, the individual is at the mercy of the ruling power and its agents. The ancient atrocities return, such as no trial by jury, confiscatory taxes on life and property, the purchasing of judges, legislators, and sheriffs; all previous forms of the prior administration of justice become part of the current machinery which administers not justice, but injustice or tyranny.

In short, all that is good rests on justice. Where there is no justice, there is no morality—no right or wrong—anything goes and usually does. Justice is a social virtue to be practiced by individuals. Justice demands that the individual reward or recognize good and condemn evil. To practice justice one should know a man for what he is and treat him accordingly, whether he be honest, dishonest, friend or thief. The good should be rewarded, the bad punished.

In this context the book will deal with general and specific principles and issues, which affect the actions of all men in society; the principles and issues will be analyzed and judged good or bad, just or unjust, accordingly. Society cannot place before it a higher or nobler goal than the administration of Justice.

To conclude, here is a bit of advice from *Conversations with Goethe,* March 22, 1825: "A great deal may be done by severity, more by love, but most by clear discernment and impartial justice."

NOTES ON JUSTICE, CHAPTER I

1. "The Spirit of Laws," *Great Books of the Western World*, Encyclopedia Britannica, Inc., Chicago, 1971, Page 1. The following authors will be referenced from the *Great Books* series: Aristotle, Marcus Aurelius Antoninus, James Boswell, Thomas Hobbes, John Locke, John Stuart Mill, Michel de Montaigne, Plato, Plutarch, Jean Jacques Rousseau, Adam Smith, Saint Augustine, Jonathan Swift.

2. IBID,P. 349.
3. IBID, P.786.
4. IBID, P. 382-85.
5. IBID,P. 609.
6. IBID,P. 481.
7. IBID, P. 382.
8. IBID, P. 384.
9. IBID, P. 506.
10. IBID, P. 92.
11. IBID
12. IBID, P. 96.
13. IBID, P. 524.
14. IBID, P. 637, Plutarch.
15. IBID, Pp. 465-66.
16. IBID, Pp. 468-69.

II

Freedom

I should have loved freedom, I believe, at all times, but in the time in which we live I am ready to worship it.
ALEXIS DE TOCQUEVILLE

Once the meaning of justice has been established, next comes the understanding of freedom and liberty, which are crucial because only under freedom can the individual achieve his highest potential and pursue his happiness.

To speak of liberty and freedom is to speak first of natural laws or the right of nature. Hobbes lays an excellent foundation of natural laws or rights. He affirms that the right of nature is the liberty each man has to use his own power for the preservation of his own life, and his own judgment and reason are the best means for achieving it. [1]

The first law of nature, according to Jean Jacques Rousseau (1712-1778), results from man's nature. "His first law is to provide for his own preservation, his first cares are those which he owes to himself; and, as soon as he reaches years of discretion, he is the sole judge of the proper means of preserving himself...." [2]

Therefore, if man's first obligation is to provide for his own life, he must live under the proper conditions in which to sustain his life, namely, liberty. By liberty is understood the absence of external impediments, the absence of opposition.

In 1772 Samuel Adams wrote a declaration of the rights of man which spoke of all the rights of mankind for all times. In addition to the natural rights of the colonists to life, liberty and property, was added the right to support and defend those rights in the best manner they could. "These are evident branches of...the duty of self-preservation, commonly called the first law of nature.... The *natural* liberty of man is to be free from any superior power on earth, and not to be under the will or legislative authority of man, but only to have the law of nature for his rule." [3]

In *The Constitution of Liberty*, Nobel-prize winner Friedrich A.

Hayek points out that liberty is a negative concept like peace. "It becomes positive only through what we make of it. It does not assure us of any particular opportunities, but leaves it to us to decide what use we shall make of the circumstances in which we find ourselves...." [4] He continues, "Liberty not only means that the individual has both the opportunity and the burden of choice; it also means that he must bear the consequences of his actions and will receive praise or blame for them. Liberty and responsibility are *inseparable.*"[5] (Emphasis added.)

From what has been discussed so far liberty seems to be extremely important, but why? Why are liberty and freedom so noble sounding and heart lifting? Why has man always been striving for liberty? Perhaps because liberty is "the parent of Virtue, Wealth and Security." [6]

To expound further, Mill explains that one cannot take away another's freedom no matter how sincerely one tries to protect another. Only by our own hands can any positive and lasting improvement in our lives be worked out. And through "the influence of these two principles all free communities have both been more exempt from social injustice and crime, and have attained more brilliant prosperity, than any others...." [7]

Furthermore, "...any restrictions on liberty reduces the number of things tried and so reduces the rate of progress. In such a society freedom of action is granted to the individual, not because it gives him greater satisfaction but because if allowed to go his own way he will on the average serve the rest of us better than any orders we know how to give." [8]

In short, liberty is the only object which benefits all alike and should provoke no sincere opposition. Liberty "is not a means to a higher political end. It is itself the highest political end," says Lord Acton. It is required for security in the pursuit of the highest objects of private life and civil society. [9]

If liberty is to live upon one's own terms and slavery is to live at the mercy of another's, then it follows that to live under one's own terms means the individual has a choice of actions. He can be virtuous or not; he can be moral. Therefore, morality requires freedom. Thus, only free men can be just men!

In his *The Road to Serfdom* , Hayek ties liberty to morality. Since morals are of necessity a phenomenon of individual conduct, to be moral one must be free to make choices. Where man is forced to act by coercion, the ability to choose has been pre-empted. Only under liberty and freedom can man be moral. As a result, only "where we ourselves are responsible for our own interests...has our decision moral value. Freedom to order our own conduct in the sphere where material circumstances force a choice upon us, and responsibility for the arrangement of our own life according to our own conscience, is the air in which alone moral sense grows and in which moral values are daily recreated in the free decision of the individual. Responsibility, not to a superior, but to one's conscience, the awareness of a duty not exacted by compulsion,... and to bear the consequences of one's own decisions, are the very essence of any morals which deserve the name." [10]

The finest thinking on freedom is offered from Albert Jay Nock's *Our Enemy The State*. Nock says that the practical reason for freedom seems to be that it is the only condition under which man can develop any kind of substantial moral fiber. Everything has been tried. Going dead against reason and experience, we have tried law, compulsion and various kinds of authoritarianism, with the result being nothing of which to be proud. The individual's desire for freedom has but one practical object, i.e., that men may become as good and decent, as elevated and noble, as they might and really wish to be. Reason, experience and observation lead to the conviction that under absolute and unqualified freedom men can, and rather promptly will, educate themselves to this desirable end; but that so long as they are to the least degree dominated by others, they never can. Nock's idea of unqualified freedom is in essence "a natural rights philosophy, a social philosophy of self-responsibility, personal creativity and development, and of unequivocal voluntarism." [11]

Algernon Sidney's (1622-1683) observation bears this out: "The glory, virtue, and power, of the Romans began and ended with their liberty." [12]

Upon hearing of President Franklin D. Roosevelt's Four Freedoms, Nock replied: "There is no such thing, four or forty. Freedom has no plural. Freedom either is, or isn't. [13]

The facts have been established thus far that man must live under liberty to become as productive, as noble, and as just as he can, since liberty is the condition under which morality thrives. Also, only the individual knows what is best for himself. And finally, liberty does not provide opportunities, but leaves the individual free to choose those actions which he thinks will best suit him and to bear the consequences of those actions.

There is one more thing to consider about freedom and liberty—the price. De Tocqueville remarked, "Some abandon freedom thinking it dangerous, others thinking it impossible." But there is a third reason. Some abandon freedom thinking it too expensive. Freedom is not free. "Those who expect to reap the blessings of freedom, must, like men, undergo the fatigues of supporting it," noted Paine.

Upon joining the Continental Army in 1776, Paine saw the need to encourage the suffering men, to remind them of the glorious cause for which they were fighting and that the price of liberty was not too high.

For these reasons, he wrote a series of articles called "Crisis," which numbered thirteen in all. In them Paine stirred the emotions of his fellow soldiers and lightened the burdens of the War and gave the men just reason and cause for their suffering and eventual victory. The first one was written on December 23, 1776 and has become one of the most cherished works of Americans. It begins, "These are the times that try men's souls. The summer soldier and the sunshine patriot will, in this crisis, shrink from the service of their country; but he that stands it *now*, deserves the love and thanks of man and woman. Tyranny, like hell, is not easily conquered; yet we have this consolation with us, that the harder the conflict, the more glorious the triumph. What we obtain too cheap, we esteem too lightly: it is dearness only that gives every thing its value. Heaven knows how to put a proper price upon its goods; and it would be strange indeed if so celestial an article as FREEDOM should not be highly rated...."

Surely once it is obtained, liberty should be closely guarded. Indeed, political jealousy in a people is a necessary and laudable passion, if not a virtue.

"Freedom is the most exacting form of civil government—it is, in fact, the most demanding state of all for man. That is because freedom demands—depends upon—self-discipline from both the governed and the governing. The foundation of freedom is self-government and the foundation of self-government is self-control," explains author Rus Walton, of *One Nation Under God.* [14] Freedom requires more, however. It requires a strong and vigilant defense. "The greater the threat of evil, the stronger that defense must be. That which is right does not survive unattended; it, too, must have its defenders....When the people of Athens sought freedom from responsibility, Athens ceased to be free." [15] A people can never be too jealous of their liberties!

Is liberty worth the effort? According to Frederic Bastiat, all you have to do is look at the entire world to decide. That is, which "countries contain the most peaceful, the most moral, and the happiest people? Those people are found in the countries where the law least interferes with private affairs; where government is least felt; where the individual has the greatest scope, and free opinion the greatest influence; where administrative powers are fewest and simplest; where taxes are lightest and most nearly equal, and popular discontent the least excited and the least justifiable; where individuals and groups most actively assume their responsibilities, and, consequently, where the morals of...human beings are constantly improving; where trade, assemblies, and associations are the least restricted;...where mankind most nearly follow its own natural inclinations;...in short, the happiest, most moral, and most peaceful people are those who most nearly follow this principle: although mankind is not perfect, still, all hope rests upon the free and voluntary actions of persons within the limits of right; law or force is to be used for nothing except the administration of universal justice.''[16]

What this means to us today is that our society, so filled with government regulations and laws, has taken away many of our liberties. For example, we cannot go into some businesses without being licensed, taxed, and regulated. We are presumed guilty (of dishonesty) until proven innocent. Our reputations are continually under attack and, for the most part, stand for nothing. Honesty and integrity have been replaced by government regulations and promises. Under this system of injustice all of us are losing.

Without their reputations to protect, some businessmen exist by government favor and subsidies. Honest ones have to compete with dishonest ones. Consumers cannot often tell the difference, buying shoddy goods only to find out too late that no one stands behind the product. Consumerism has sprung up as a response to bad business practices. But the problem is not always the businessmen; it is the system.

Government interference has corrupted the system by assuming the responsibilities that belong rightfully to both sellers and buyers. Manhattan Supreme Court Justice Burton B. Roberts, for instance, freed without fine or penalty, the head of the nation's largest beef company *after* he was found guilty of bribery-conspiracy charges because the judge realized that to do business in New York the company had to join ''the corrupt system.''

Under a free system corruption cannot exist and prosper. Freedom and liberty bring out the best qualities in mankind. All benefit—businessmen and consumers alike. But first, we must have the freedom in which to make choices and to assume the responsibility of our choices; in addition, government should not be permitted to subsidize one group over another. Freedom reinforces the pride one takes in himself as a free man or woman, that one can stand on his own two feet, practicing the virtue of independence.

What better way to summarize the spirit of liberty and to end this chapter than by this quote from the Last Will and Testament of Josiah Quincy, Jr., 1774: ''I give to my son, when he shall arrive to the age of fifteen years, Algernon Sidney's works,—John Locke's works,—Lord Bacon's works,—Gordon's *Tacitus*,—and *Cato's Letters.* May the spirit of liberty rest upon him!''

NOTES ON FREEDOM AND LIBERTY, CHAPTER II

1. IBID, P. 86.
2. IBID, P. 388.
3. *The Annals of America,* (Chicago: Encyclopedia Britannica, Inc., 1968), Volume 3, P. 217.
4. A Gateway Edition, (Chicago: Henry Regnery Co., 1972), P. 19.
5. IBID, P. 71.
6. *Essays on Liberty, Civil and Religious, and other Important Subjects*, John Trenchard and Thomas Gordon, Da Capo Press, New York, 1971, Volumes I and II, *Cato's Letters*, No. 25.
7. Op. cit., P. 346.
8. Phillips, H.G., Op cit., P. 9.
9. *Essays on Freedom and Power,* (Cleveland, Ohio: The World Publishing Co., 1972), by arrangement with the Macmillan Co., P. 74.
10. (Chicago: The University of Chicago Press, 1969), Pp. 211-12.
11. (New York: Free Life Editions, 1973), Pp. xi, 98-9.
12. *Discourses Concerning Government*, 3rd Edition, MDCCLI, republished, Gregg International Publishers, Ltd., England, 1968.
13. *Selected Letters of Albert Jay Nock*, Collected and edited by Francis J. Nock, (Caldwell, Ohio: The Caxton Printers, Ltd., 1962), P. 199.
14. (Old Tappan, New Jersey: Fleming H. Revell Co., 1975), P. 51.
15. IBID, Pp. 282-83.
16. *The Law*, (Irvington-on-the-Hudson, New York: The Foundation for Economic Education, Inc., 1974), P. 73.

III

Tyranny

If people cannot expect redress to public evils, if they will tamely suffer a fall from rich to poor, they can expect a worse fate, from That to Slavery.
CATO'S LETTERS, NO. 3, NOVEMBER 19, 1720

It is important to understand tyranny, the opposite of justice and freedom, because the change from freedom into tyranny usually occurs so slowly that most people are unaware of it.

When man emerged from the Dark Ages, all self-imposed rulers started to become suspect. Then when terms such as self-rule, constitutional law, representative government, and individual, natural rights came into use, when as de Tocqueville said, "No one renders obedience to man, but to justice and law," all forms of non-elected governments were held in contempt. The era of The Divine Right of Kings was over. Nearly every form of non-elected government was suspect. Czars, emperors and kings were considered to be despots, tyrants, or usurpers to some extent.

John Locke (1632-1704) begins the discussion on tyranny with his premise that slavery is opposed to natural law because "The natural liberty of man is to be free from any superior power on earth, and not to be under the will or legislative authority of man, but to have only the law of Nature for his rule.... A liberty to follow my own will...not to be subject to the inconstant, uncertain, unknown, arbitrary will of another man.... This freedom from absolute, arbitrary power is so necessary to, and closely joined with, a man's preservation that he cannot part with it but by what forfeits his preservation and life together."[1] In short, slavery is inimical to life itself.

Usurpation, says Locke, is where one (or more than one) has taken the possession of what another has a right to. For example, if someone takes over government from the rightful ruler, the right to rule has been usurped. But an usurper can never have right on his side.

When it comes to defining tyranny, Locke put it this way: "As usurpation is the exercise of power which another hath a right to, so tyranny is the exercise of power beyond right, which nobody can have a right to." Whereas nobody has a right to the life, liberty and property of another, any infringement of these rights becomes tyranny. "Wherever the power that is put in any hands for the government of the people and the preservation of their properties is applied to other ends, and made use of to impoverish, harass, or subdue them to the arbitrary and irregular commands of those that have it, there it presently becomes tyranny, whether those that thus use it are one or many."[2] In short, if individual rights are not respected, but instead violated, usurpation becomes tyranny.

Algernon Sidney was an English republican and political theorist who served for a time in Parliament. He is remembered for his famous *Discourses Concerning Government,* which although written between 1680 and 1683, was not published until 1698, after his death.

Sidney was arrested, tried, and convicted for complicity in the Rye House Plot in 1683. In actuality, the charge was treason, for which he was promptly beheaded. His *Discourses,* which was still in manuscript form at that time, was used against him. The indictment cited sentences saying that the King is subject to law and is responsible to the people, and may be deposed as a "false, seditious, and traitorous libel." He also cited the principles that all people have a natural right to govern themselves; they can choose their rulers as they see fit; government derives its power from the people, and may be held accountable to them.

Although his writings are clear and forceful, Sidney had a greater influence on American colonists because of his life, trial and subsequent martyrdom. In France, he was ranked along with Washington, Franklin, Voltaire, and Rousseau. In America, many patriots who had never read *Discourses,* appealed to Sidney's memory as a symbol of defiance to tyrants.

In his writings, Sidney has a simple way of defining tyranny. He says that the "liberty of man cannot be limited or diminshed by one, or any number of men, and none can give away the right of another." Any individual or group who did, would be a robber, pirate, and usurper. Sidney added that to depend upon the will of another man is slavery, as a slave cannot dispose of his person or his property. Someone once called a slave one who waits for someone else to free him.

The authors of *Cato's Letters* were John Trenchard and Thomas Gordon. John Trenchard, a squire of ample means, was an Old Whig pamphleteer who was an extreme liberal, in the true and original sense of the word as far back as the Exclusion Crisis of 1679. Thomas Gordon, many years younger than Trenchard, was an ambitious and successful Scottish journalist.

Together they collaborated on a series of articles signed "Cato" that appeared in *The London Journal* and *The British Journal. Later* those writings were collected into a four-volume book called *Cato's Letters.* They numbered 144 pieces and were originally published between November, 1720 and December, 1723. The articles were "among the most troublesome thorns that pricked the vulnerable sides of the British ministry."

Cato's Letters were a searing indictment of eighteenth-century English politics and society, written in response to the South Sea Bubble crisis. They also denounced standing armies. In the American colonies, the writings of Trenchard and Gordon ranked with the treatises of Locke as the most authoritive statement of the nature of political liberty.

Cato's Letters have much to say on the subject of slavery and tyranny. Letter No. 10 argues that one oppression cannot be supported but by another, and a greater; and force and violence alone can do what reason cannot and will not do. Regarding usurpation, No. 11 claims that the sole end of men's entering into political societies was mutual protection and defense; and whatever power does not contribute to those purposes is not government, but usurpation. No. 59 states that governments are instituted for the good of society; that when they cease they become usurpation; and No. 63 claims that liberty produces virtue, happiness, moral excellency, politeness, arts and science; whereas tyranny produces wickedness, tyranny, corruption, baseness, destruction of everything valuable, desirable, and noble. They conclude by saying that the state of tyranny is a state of war, which concurs with Thomas Aquinas who said, "Tyrannical government is altogether corrupt."

Rousseau wrote about the collapse of liberty in a republic and the rise of despotism, which was brought about by certain magistrates. They fomented everything that might weaken men united in society by promoting dissension among them, everything that might sow the seeds of division while giving society the air of harmony, and everything that might inspire the different ranks of people with mutual hatred and distrust, but setting the rights and interests of one against those of another, and so strengthening the power which comprehended them all.

It is from the midst of this disorder and these revolutions, that despotism would at length trample on both the laws and the people, and establish itself on the ruins of the republic, and the people would no longer have either chiefs or laws, but only tyrants. From this moment there would be no question of virtue or morality; for despotism, wherever it prevails, admits no other master; it no sooner appears than blind obedience is the only virtue which slaves can still practice.[3]

During the American Revolutionary period, there was a great volume of writing on tyranny, slavery, oppression, and despotism. Madison declared in *The Federalist*: "The accumulation of all powers, legislative, executive, and judiciary, in the same hands,whether hereditary, self-appointed, or elective, may justly be pronounced the very definition of tyranny." He reinforced his point by quoting Jefferson's dictum that concentrating "all the powers of government...in the same hands, is precisely the definition of despotic government."

Madison warned the people to be on guard. They must themselves be the final barrier to tyranny, he said, for "a mere demarcation on parchment of the constitutional limits of the several departments is not a sufficient guard against those encroachments which lead to a tyrannical concentration of all the powers of government in the same hands. There are more instances of the abridgement of the freedom of the people by gradual and silent encroachments of those in power than by violent and sudden usurpations."

Jefferson understood political slavery better than most of his contemporaries. He saw the eventual result of Britain's parliamentary acts as nothing less than slavery for the colonists. He concluded: "Single acts of tyranny may be ascribed to the accidental opinion of a day; but a series of oppressions, begun at a distinguished period, and pursued, unalterably through every change of ministers, too plainly prove a deliberate and systemical plan of reducing us to slavery." Jefferson knew as experience has shown, "that even under the best forms [of government], those entrusted with power have, in time, and by slow operations, perverted it into tyranny."

In full agreement, the wise Sam Adams writes that governors have no right to seek and take what they please; by this, instead of being content with the station assigned them, that of honorable servants of the society, they would soon become absolute masters, despots, and tyrants.

Hamilton summed it up when he said, "In the general course of human nature, *a power over a man's substance amounts to a power over his will.*"

Although writers today have witnessed the end of most of the governments of kings, tyrants, and despots in western cultures, slavery still exists, albeit with another master. Herbert Spencer (1820-1903), a famous libertarian writer of the nineteenth century, calls modern-day slavery socialism. He maintains that all socialism involves slavery, since a slave is one who labors under coercion to satisfy another's desires,[4] whether it be a Five-Year Plan, arbitrary government regulations, or income taxation.

Hayek says that the individual under socialism "is forced to act not according to a coherent plan of his own but to serve the ends of others.... He is unable either to use his own intelligence or knowledge or to follow his own aims and beliefs.... Coercion is evil precisely because it thus eliminates an individual as a thinking and valuing person and makes him a bare tool in the achievement of the ends of another."[5]

The word socialism brings up another term that could be construed to mean slavery, that of "planning." For when a plan is somebody else's, individual freedom has been eliminated. Hayek claims that socialism is a step backward in history to tyranny. He says that furthermore it must not be forgotten how socialism has persuaded liberal-minded people to submit once more to that regimentation of economic life which they had overthrown. In the words of Adam Smith, socialism puts governments in a position where "to support themselves they are obliged to be oppressive and tyrannical."

While "planning" is the opposite of individual freedom, socialism is a form of tyranny where society exploits its members in the name of society. In other words, there is no such thing as planning for freedom, only for tyranny. The crucial point is that individual freedom cannot be reconciled with the supremacy of one single purpose to which the whole society is to be subordinated. In a free society, people plan their own lives; under socialism, the government plans it for them. And thus, tyranny slips in via the back-door approach, under the guise of "the good of society," "for the national welfare," etc.

There are numerous new forms of despotism: administrative, legal, bureaucratic, governmental, and majorital. There is also the despotism of society, of the state, and of special interest groups. In a letter to Madison dated March 15, 1789, Jefferson aired his concern over legislative and executive tyranny: "The executive power in our government is not only, perhaps not even the principal, object of my solicitude. The tyranny of the legislature is really the danger most to be feared, and will continue to be so for many years to come. The tyranny of the executive power will come in its turn, but at a more distant period," (*e.g.* executive orders). In short, despotism and tyranny are simply the violation of an individual's rights, for any reason whatsoever.

There seems to be universal agreement on how tyrants stay in power. Plato enumerates a tyrant's desperate measures as stirring up of foreign wars to smother domestic discord, assassinations of enemies, purging of friends or followers, confiscation of property, and generally indiscriminate blood-letting. Hamilton writes that the resort to unwarranted searches and seizures (which the U.S. Treasury allows), the creation of *ex post facto* (which the I.R.S. permits), and the arrest and punishment of men without trial "have been in all ages the favorite and most formidable instruments of tyranny." The end purpose in all cases is the same—success in the effort to gain and keep power. The means are, generally, force and fraud.

Aristotle gave advice to tyrants on how to maintain their power: Sow discord among the subjects, impoverish them by multiplying taxes, employ informers, and encourage the betrayal of one faction by another. This is sound advice for all forms of tyranny and it has been followed for centuries with proven success.

Please note, however, the total absence of any virtues—justice, honesty, integrity, loyalty, and trust—under tyranny and despotism. It is truly an oppressive society. About the only good thing to be said about a tyrannical government is, it seems to be the shortest lived, which suggests that might without right is an inherently weak system.

Today we all suffer at the hands of those who would divide and conquer in order to stay in power. For instance, many citizens see prostitution, pornography, drugs, homosexuality, and gambling as evils that should be routed from society at all cost. Thus, we have the proliferation of laws, law enforcers, and criminals. The courts are saturated with cases to be tried and the prisons are flowing over. Here again, one must ask, where does the responsibility for this situation lie? Upon honest reflection, one must conclude that these "society crimes" are really individual choices and not the business of the public justice system. They are "victimless crimes" in which the public can suffer only indirectly. The real victim is the participating individual, who should be free to make his own decisions and be responsible for them.

By interfering in other people's affairs, we have created a type of tyranny whereby some individual's rights are being infringed upon by society, and the innocent suffer because the justice system is too busy punishing imprudent individuals, rather than punishing the real criminals—murderers, burglars, rapists, etc.

Again we see a corrupt system where all lose. While we are being polarized against each other, society is breaking down. Life and property are not being protected. And tyranny gains ground. It is a question of seeking the truth, maybe seeing the problem from another's point of view, or at least being willing to do "what is right." All honest men should be able to agree on what is just.

Thus, we conclude with a bit of advice from John Locke who warned men that they could never be secure from tyranny if there were no means to escape it till they were under it; and, therefore, they have not only a right to get out of it, but to prevent it.

NOTES ON TYRANNY, CHAPTER III

1. Op. Cit., Pp. 29-30.
2. IBID, P. 71.
3. IBID, P. 361.
4. *The Man Versus The State*, Introduction by Albert Jay Nock, (Caldwell, Idaho: The Caxton Printers, Ltd., 1969), P. 41.
5. Op. Cit., P. 21.

IV

Property Rights

No private rights are so unimportant that they can be surrendered with impunity to the caprices of a government.
ALEXIS DE TOCQUEVILLE

This chapter is crucial because it discusses the question of whether man is truly free and competent to run his own life, or whether he needs to be looked after and taken care of by his government. It depends on how one sees man, as good and just or depraved and unworthy. Since an individual's person is also property, the right to property includes the right to use or abuse one's person without governmental or societal interference—to be free. Here is what some liberty-loving writers have said about property rights.

Sidney writes that nations should be well informed of their rights, is of the most absolute necessity, because the happiness or infelicity of any people entirely depends upon the enjoyment or deprivation of those rights.

In Letter No. 62, *Cato* says, "Let People alone, and they will take Care of themselves, and do it best; and if they do not, a sufficient Punishment will follow their Neglect, without the Magistrate's Interposition and Penalties." In full agreement, de Tocqueville said that every individual is the best judge of his own interest.

Jefferson never doubted the efficacy of the human mind. When Virginia passed a bill based on Jefferson's *Statute of Virginia for Religious Freedom,* he remarked: "It is comfortable to see the standard of reason at length erected, after so many ages during which the human mind has been held in vassalage by kings, priests and nobles: and it is honorable for us to have produced the first legislature who had the courage to declare that the reason of man may be trusted with the formation of his own opinions."

In *On Liberty*, Mill has an excellent discourse on what individuality and individual rights actually mean. He says that the individual is not accountable to society for his actions, in so far as these concern the interests of no person but himself. The sole reason for which mankind are justified, individually or collectively, in interfering with the liberty of any of their number is self-protection. The only purpose for which power can be rightfully exercised over any member of the community, against his will, is to prevent harm to others. His own good, either physical or moral, is not a sufficient reason. He cannot rightfully be compelled to do or forbear because it will make him happier, because, in the opinions of others, to do so would be wise, or even right. The only part of the conduct of any one, for which he is answerable to society, is that which concerns others. In the part which merely concerns himself, his independence is, of right, *absolute.* Over himself, over *his own body and mind, the individual is sovereign.*[1] (Emphasis added.)

Mill continues, "No society in which these liberties are not, on the whole, respected, is free....The only freedom which deserves the name, is that of pursuing our own good in our own way, so long as we do not attempt to deprive others of theirs, or impede their efforts to obtain it, even though they should think our conduct foolish, perverse, or wrong. Each is the proper guardian of his own health, whether bodily, *or* mental and spiritual. Mankind are greater gainers by suffering each other to live as seems good to themselves, than by compelling each to live as seems good to the rest."[2]

If people are restrained in things affecting their own good, they can be dulled and blunted. To give any fair play to the nature of each individual, it is essential that different persons should be allowed to lead different lives. It is only the cultivation of individuality which produces, or can produce, well-developed human beings, the end result being that it brings human beings themselves nearer to the best they can be.

Besides, adds Mill, "I am not aware that any community has a right to force another to be civilised."[3]

Leaving men free to be themselves is the *essence* of freedom. But freedom is attainable only in communities where rights are sacred, and law is supreme. This is because "If one man's rights are infringed, no other man obtains them; on the contrary, all men are thereby threatened with a similar injury."[4]

By far the best discourse on this subject is entitled "Man's Rights," written by Ayn Rand in her book, *The Virtue of Selfishness.* The reasons why Rand is the only person to discuss individual rights so completely is that 1) It is a fairly new concept, discovered around the 1770s, and 2) Most writers take rights for granted, without giving them a moral base. It is the moral basis under individual rights that explains the crucial role they play in society.

"'Rights'," says Rand, "are a moral concept—the concept that provides a logical transition from the principles guiding an individual's actions to the principles guiding his relationship with others—the concept that preserves and protects individual morality in a social context—the link between the moral code of a man and the legal code of a society, between ethics and politics. *Individual rights are the means of subordinating society to moral law....* The principle of man's individual rights represented the extension of morality into the social system—as a limitation of the power of the state, as man's protection against the brute force of the collective, as the subordination of might to right."

Rand continues by defining what a "right" is and on what it is based. She says, "A 'right' is a moral principle defining and sanctioning a man's freedom of action in a social context. There is only *one* fundamental right.... a man's right to his own life. Life is a process of self-sustaining and self-generated action; the right to life...[is] the freedom to take all the actions required by the nature of a rational being for the support, the furtherance, the fulfillment and the enjoyment of his own life. (Such is the meaning of the right to life, liberty and the pursuit of happiness.)... To violate man's rights means to compel him to act against his own judgment, or to expropriate his values."[5]

If the one fundamental right is the right to life, then the right to property is the implementation of that right. Therefore, all the laws which constitute the powers and the form of government are less important and have less influence on the happiness of nations than those which constitute property rights. Thus, to be free, government's coercive powers must be fixed and subordinated on one side, while individual property is secured on the other.

An extension of the right to property is the proprietary right one holds to his own person. Nobody has any right to his own person but the individual himself. The labor of one's body and the work of one's hands are properly one's own. Only the individual has a right to his own labor's product, to which nobody else can have access without permission. Without this reservation, the individual has no property rights at all.

As a consequence of property rights, Locke points out the right of freedom to one's person, a right with which everyone is born and which no other man has a power over, yields a second right: that before any other man, he has the right to inherit, with his brethren, his father's property.[6]

It becomes obvious, then, that any man who violates the rights of another can never have a right to his property as robbers and pirates never have a right to their booty.

Montesquieu goes so far as to say that society has no right to an individual's property, for "whenever the public good happens to be the matter in question, it is not for the advantage of the public to deprive an individual of his property, or even to retrench the least part of it by law, or a political regulation.... Thus when the public has occasion for the estate of an individual, it ought never to act by the rigour of political law."[7]

Rousseau places the right to property equally as high as liberty itself because it implies all other rights and is the most sacred of all the rights of citizenship, as it more nearly affects the preservation of life; as property is the true foundation of civil society, it is the real guarantee of the undertakings of citizens.[8]

When it comes to securing property rights, Paine, in his "Dissertation of First Principles of Government," July, 1795, believed that the best security for property, be it much or little, is to remove from every part of the community every cause of complaint and every motive of violence, which can only be done by an equality of rights. When rights are secure, property is secure. But when property is made a pretense for unequal or exclusive rights, it weakens the right to hold the property, and provokes envy, dissension, and distrust. There is no way that some property can be secure while other property is being confiscated. Examples of this are conscription and income taxation laws; both negate the right to life (and property).

"As property, honestly obtained, is best secured by an equality of rights," says Paine, "so ill-gotten property depends for protection on a monopoly of rights. He who has robbed another of his property, will next endeavor to disarm him of his rights, to secure that property; for when the robber becomes the legislator he believes himself secure." This is called "legalizing theft." But theft by any other name (egalitarianism, equality, socialism, etc.) is still theft.

An essay appeared by James Madison in the *National Gazette* on March 27, 1792, entitled: "The Right to Property and Property in Rights." It is one of Madison's finest works, and thus we excerpt parts of it here. It maintains that since

> Government is instituted to protect property of every sort,... that alone is a just government which impartially secures to every man whatever is his *own.*
>
> That is not a just government, nor is property secured under it, where the property which a man has in his personal safety and personal liberty is violated by arbitrary seizures of one class of citizens for the service of the rest.
>
> A just security to property is not afforded by that government under which unequal taxes oppress one species of property and reward another species; where arbitrary taxes invade the domestic sanctuaries of the rich and excessive taxes grind the faces of the poor;
>
> If the United States means to obtain or deserve the full

> praise due to wise and just governments, they will equally respect the rights of property and the property in rights.[9]

Lord Acton summed it up when he said that a people averse to the institution of private property is without the first element of freedom.

It should be obvious by now that private property and freedom are necessary to each other. Hayek reminds us that private property is the most important guarantee of freedom, not only for those who own property, but also for those who do not. It is only because the control of the means of production is divided among many people acting independently (free-enterprise) that nobody has complete power over us, that we as individuals can decide what to do with our lives.

Property rights are crucial because as Rand says, "Without property rights, no other rights are possible.... The man who produces while others dispose of his product, is a slave."[10] Furthermore, property is an appendage of liberty, notes Sidney.

One of the key tests of the security of private property is the government's attitude toward money. A hard currency of gold and silver, which keeps its value, is what preserves the value of property. But a depreciating currency renders all property, including life, unstable, open to the whims and caprices of government manipulation. In Sparta, for example, gold and silver money were prohibited. The government wished to reduce the nation to a dead level of poverty and keep it that way. It succeeded.

Another test is that of inheritance laws. High estate taxes are a reversion to the medieval days of serfdom when a deceased's property is "gifted" to the state, or directly confiscated by taxes. Hence, the government acquires once-owned private property of large land parcels, parks, etc. The end result must be that all land will end up in the hands of the few or managed by the government. The majority of the people will become serfs working for others. This problem is being accelerated today by regional planning laws, called Regionalism. Few things can be done with one's property without the "permission and consent" of some governmental board. The extent of this modern usurpation is discussed in Chapter 19.

In a free society it is paramount that inequality of property be maintained. Not only is it certain that property will be unequal, observed Paine, but industry, superiority of talents, dexterity of management, extreme frugality, fortunate opportunities, or the opposite, will always produce that effect.

Property is the fruit of labor; it is desirable, a positive good in the world. That some should be rich shows that others may become rich, and it is encouraging to the less fortunate to think that they may become more fortunate.

To summarize, one's person and one's material possessions are property. Property rights are the implementation of the right to life. All violations of the right to property are violations to one's life. A just government respects and protects both. Any violations of such rights by government is tyranny. And, finally, mankind is the better for it when individuals are left alone to run their own lives.

"The chief care of a good government should be to teach people little by little to do without it." (De Tocqueville, *Journey to America,* p. 15)

NOTES ON PROPERTY RIGHTS, CHAPTER IV

1. Op. Cit., P. 271.
2. IBID., P. 297.
3. *Constitution of Liberty*, P. 530.
4. Isabel Paterson, *The God of the Machine*, (Caldwell, Idaho: The Caxton Printers, Ltd., 1968), P. 93.
5. Reprinted in *Capitalism: The Unknown Ideal*, (New York: The New American Library, 1966), Pp. 286-89.
6. Op. Cit., P. 69.
7. Op. Cit., P. 221.
8. Op. Cit., P. 377.
9. *Annals of America*, Vol. 3, Pp. 498-99.
10. Op. Cit., P. 288.

V

Government

...A wise and frugal government, which shall restrain men from injuring one another, which shall leave them otherwise free to regulate their own pursuits of industry and improvement, and shall not take from the mouth of labor the bread it has earned. This is the sum of good government....
THOMAS JEFFERSON, FIRST INAUGURAL ADDRESS, MARCH 4, 1801

The discussion on government begins with Aristotle, who realized that the same things are best both for individuals and for governments, and these are the things which the legislator ought to implant in the minds of his citizens.[1]

Locke adds that the chief aim of men uniting under a government is the preservation of their property—to secure every man's possession of the things of this life. And, therefore, the government ought not to take away these wordly things, *not even by law.*[2] For "whenever the legislators endeavor to take away and destroy the property of the people, they put themselves in a state of war with the people, who are thereupon absolved from any further obedience...."[3] In short, government does away with its own reason for existence when it violates its citizens' rights.

Montesquieu warned that the real wants of the people ought never to give way to the imaginary wants of the state. Imaginary wants are those which flow from the passions and the weakness of the governors, for extraordinary projects, or inordinate desires of glory.

Rousseau also warns us that the pretext of the public good is always the most dangerous scourge of the people. Every government tends to become lax. The nation becomes involved in debt and the people oppressed, while the government can do very little with a great deal of money.

When it comes to choosing the men who are to run the government, Jonathan Swift, in his *Gulliver's Travels,* has some words of wisdom. The Lilliputians, says Swift, have more regard to good morals than to great abilities. Providence never intended to make the management of public affairs a mystery, to be comprehended only by a few persons of sublime genius, of which there seldom are three born in an age. But they suppose truth and justice to be in every man's power; the practice of which virtues, assisted by experience and a good intention, would qualify any man for the service of his country.[4]

To put it in its proper perspective, governments are not set up for the advantage, profit, pleasure, or glory of one or a few men, but for the good of society.

Sidney says that a good magistrate encourages justice, virtue, honesty and generally advances everything that tends to increase the valor, strength, greatness and happiness of the nation, creating a good union among them, and bringing every man to an exact understanding of his rights. Thus we are establishing some standards by which to judge our present governmental officials.

Cato's Letters, No. 25, says that since the good of the governed is the sole end of government, that the greatest and best governors are those who make their people great and happy; and they the worst, who make their people little, wicked and miserable. Again, justice is seen as the prime virtue of good government, as well as the standard by which to judge the efficacy of government.

It seems that of all the sciences, government is the most important, the easiest to know and the least understood. But everyone can tell whether he lives under a good government, if the fruits of his labor are his to keep, and if he enjoys them in peace and security. Therefore, men have a right to expect protection and liberty and the responsibility to oppose rapine and tyranny whenever exercised.

It was not until the late 1700s that the real essence of government was discovered. Paine, for instance, wrote prolifically on the subject of government. He said that government should be like nature, for the more simple the thing is, the less liable it is to be disordered, and the easier it is repaired when disordered. In "Crisis X," written March 5, 1782, Paine said, "A government or an administration, who means and acts honestly, has nothing to fear, and consequently has nothing to conceal." The public ought to elect men into government who will at once throw aside the narrow prejudices of party and make the good of the whole the ruling object of their conduct.

In his "Dissertation on First Principles of Government," Paine reminds us that there is no subject more interesting to every man than the subject of government, because his security, whether he be rich or poor, is connected with it. It is, therefore, in his interest as well as his duty to make himself acquainted with its principles and what the practice ought to be.

Paine strips away the mystery surrounding governments. He claims, "The more perfect civilization is, the less occasion has it for government, because the more does it regulate its own affairs, and govern itself." How often, Paine adds, is the natural propensity of society disturbed or destroyed by the operations of government. When the government assumes to exist for itself, it acts by partialities, thus becoming the cause of the mischiefs it ought to prevent.

Jefferson, ever wise and practical, believed that government should depend for justification upon its utility for the governed and upon their consent. He maintained, "The whole art of government consists in the art of being honest," because "No government ought to be without censors...." He also warned the populace of the dangers of encroaching governments, for it is the natural progress of things for liberty to yield and government to gain ground.

Mill had the same doubts about government. He declared that, "Leaving things to the Government, like leaving them to Providence, is synonymous with caring nothing about them, and accepting their results, when disagreeable, as visitations of Nature."[5]

There are three things wrong with leaving things to the government to do: 1) The thing to be done is likely to be better done by individuals, 2) It is desirable that it should be done by them as a means to their own education, and 3) There is a great evil in adding unnecessarily to governmental power. Hence Mill succinctly summarizes his view of the purpose of government: "Security of person and property, and equal justice between individuals, are the first needs of society, and the primary ends of government."[6] *The Federalist,* No. 51, expressed a similar opinion: "Justice is the end of government. It is the end of civil society."

Alexis de Tocqueville (1805-1859), a famous French philosopher, wrote extensively on the subject of government. He discovered that when public employments are few in number, ill-paid, and precarious, while the different kinds of business are numerous and lucrative, it is to business and not to government that the new and eager ones turn. But if business is crippled by regulations and hopes of a successful future are checked, men rush to the head of the state to relieve their own necessities at the cost of the public treasury.[7]

From his study of the United States in the 1830s, de Tocqueville conceived of his idea of an ideal society: "I can conceive of a society in whch all men would feel an equal love and respect for the laws of which they consider themselves the author; in which the authority of the government would be respected as necessary, not divine; and in which the loyalty of the subject to the chief magistrate would not be a passion, but a quiet and rational persuasion. With every individual in the possession of rights which he is sure to retain, a kind of manly confidence and reciprocal courtesy would arise; the community would be protected from tyranny and license.''[8]

One of the happiest consequences of the absence of government, observed de Tocqueville, is the strengthening of individual virtue, which never fails to follow therefrom. ''Each man learns to think and to act for himself without counting on the support of any outside power which, however watchful it be, can never answer all the needs of man in society.''[9]

A system of government that is guided by principles is the cornerstone of liberty. The reason for this is that freedom will not be destroyed by piecemeal encroachments, but preserved by principles overriding all acts of legislation. In the 1920s and 1930s the trend of the time was to establish governments of trust in men, which was contrary to all the beliefs of the Founding Fathers. It was Jefferson who warned, for example, that "free government is founded in jealousy, not in confidence.... In questions of power, then, let no more be heard of confidence in man, but bind him down from mischief by the chains of the Constitution.''

The history of mankind has repeatedly shown the struggle of the individual against the state. One should ask by now where does government obtain its power? All the power government has is given it by society, or else it is usurped from time to time on one pretext or another; there is no other source from which power can be drawn. Just as the government has no money of its own, so it has no power of its own. Therefore, every assumption of governmental power, whether by gift or seizure, leaves society with so much less power; there is never, nor can be, any strengthening of governmental power without a corresponding and roughly equivalent depletion of social power.

This exchange of power is continually flowing back and forth. Around 1776, the direction was mainly toward the individual. Since then, governments have been receiving more and more power at the individual's expense. When the government of the United States in the 1930s announced that it was its responsibility and function to provide jobs for all Americans, astute students of history saw it as merely a proposal for enhancing its own power. In 1794 Madison called it ''the old trick of turning every contingency into a resource for accumulating force in the government.'' By accepting progressively more responsibility for the individual's life, the government also accepts the corresponding power over his life. Thus individual rights become subordinated to governmental power and accepted by society.

By far the best discourse on government comes from Rand's article entitled ''The Nature of Government.'' She says that by abolishing the use of aggressive force in the hands of the individual and placing it in the hands of government, a monopoly is created. Its purpose is to place retaliatory force under objective control—under objectively defined laws.

Because government holds this monopoly on force, it is vital that its actions be rigidly defined, delimited and circumscribed. If a society is to be free, its government must be controlled.

As was mentioned in the chapter on individual rights, the individual should be legally free to take any action he pleases (except that of violating another's rights), while a government official is bound by law in his every official act. "A private individual may do anything except that which is legally *forbidden*; a government official may do nothing except that which is legally *permitted*. This is the means of subordinating 'might' to 'right.' This is the American concept of 'a government of laws and not of men.' "[10]

This concept of government is derived from the nature and purpose of a proper government. The basic principle of both is stated in the Declaration of Independence: "to secure these rights, governments are instituted among men, deriving their just powers from the consent of the governed...."

This means that the government is not the ruler, but the servant of the citizens. It has *no* rights, only the power that society gives it or that it illegally usurps.

Rand maintains that there are three broad categories which are the proper function of a government, "all of them involving the issues of physical force and the protection of men's rights: *the police*, to protect men from criminals—*the armed services*, to protect men from foreign invaders—*the law courts*, to settle disputes among men according to objective laws."[11]

But the essential point to remember is that the purpose of government is to protect individual rights. This understanding of government is fairly new, having been discovered only two hundred years ago. The Founding Fathers' genius culminated in the Constitution which, to repeat, puts a limitation on the government, not on private citizens—"that it does not prescribe the conduct of private individuals, only the conduct of the government—that it is not a charter *for* government power, but a charter of the citizens' protection *against* government."[12]

But when government turns on its people, it creates a nightmare: "...a government that *initiates* the employment of force against men who had forced no one, the employment of armed compulsion against disarmed victims, is a nightmare infernal machine designed to annihilate morality: such a government reverses its only moral purpose and switches from the role of protector to the role of man's deadliest enemy, from the role of policeman to the role of a criminal vested with the right to the wielding of violence against victims deprived of the right of self-defense."[13]

To conclude, here is a statement made fifty years ago by the far-sighted H.L. Mencken (1880-1956) describing the government then in power: "It [the State] has taken on a vast mass of new duties and responsibilities; it has spread out its powers until they penetrate to every act of the citizen, however secret; it has begun to throw around its operations the high dignity and impeccability of a State religion; its agents become a separate and superior caste, with authority to bind and loose, and their thumbs in every pot. But it still remains, as it was in the beginning the common enemy of all well-disposed industrious and decent men."

Compare this to the quote by Thomas Jefferson opening this chapter. What a difference in only 125 years! It is time to put government back in the place of servant, not master.

In Letter No. 48, *Cato* hit the nail on the head when he argued that only government founded on liberty is a blessing—otherwise it is a curse!

NOTES ON GOVERNMENT, CHAPTER V

1. Op. Cit., P. 538.
2. Op. Cit., Pp. 16-17.
3. IBID, P. 76.
4. Op. Cit., Pp. 28-29.
5. Op. Cit., P. 343.
6. IBID, P. 422.
7. *Democracy in America*, (New York: Alfred A. Knopf, 1945, Volume II), Pp. 249-50.
8. *Democracy in America*, (New York: Alfred A. Knopf, 1945, Volume I), The Henry Reeve Text, P. 9.
9. *Journey to America*, translated by George Lawrence, Edited by J.P. Mayer, (New Haven, Conn.: Yale University, 1960), P. 51.
10. Op. Cit., P. 298.
11. IBID, P. 300.
12. IBID, P. 302.
13. Ayn Rand, *Atlas Shrugged*, (New York: Random House, 1957), P. 1063.

VI

Revolution

That to secure these rights, governments are instituted among men,.. that, whenever any form of government becomes destructive of these ends, it is the right of the people to alter or abolish it, and to institute a new government.... [When a people suffer] a long train of abuses and usurpations...it is their right, it is their duty, to throw off such government, and to provide new guards for their security.
DECLARATION OF INDEPENDENCE

The tree of liberty must be refreshed from time to time, with the blood of patriots and tyrants. It is its natural manure.
THOMAS JEFFERSON, JULY 6, 1763

A chapter on revolutions following one on governments is quite natural, since they usually follow that order in reality. Once it lays the groundwork from the ancient writers, this chapter will concentrate on the world's only successful revolution—the American Revolution. Because revolutions are a result of economic and political inequities, perhaps as bad as those we are witnessing today, it is important to study their causes and effects, for they are far from being a thing of the past.

In *Laws VI*, Plato observes that man should never submit to tyranny; if there is no other way, he must flee the "yoke of slavery." And "if at last necessity plainly compels him to be an outlaw from his native land, rather than bow his neck to the yoke of slavery...he must...endure all such trials, rather than accept another form of government, which is likely to make men worse."[1]

Aristotle says, "The happy life is thought to be virtuous; now a virtuous life requires exertion.... For happiness [lies]...in virtuous activities."[2] Since it is not virtuous to live under a tyrannical system of government and take no action, one must take a stand for that which is right. To have the courage of one's convictions is a virtue. As Henry Clay said in the House of Representatives on March 24, 1818, "All oppressed people are authorized, whenever they can, to rise and break their fetters." In agreement is Thomas Aquinas, who says it is proper to overthrow a tyrannical government because it is directed, not to the common good, but to the private good of the rulers.... There is no sedition in disturbing a government of this kind....''[3]

Sidney, in explaining his views on rebellions, maintains that an oppressed people, by rebelling, cannot commit a crime by vindicating their own liberty. ''The general revolt of a nation cannot be called a rebellion,'' since a rebellion is, to say the least, superior to tyranny and unopposed oppression!

In his *A Letter Concerning Toleration*, Locke writes that natural law and reason will provoke man to rise up against tyranny. He admits that since it is very difficult for men patiently to suffer while they are stripped of the goods which they have got by their honest industry, ''what else can be expected but that these men...should in the end think it lawful for them to resist force with force, and to defend their natural rights...with arms as well as they can? That this has been hitherto the ordinary course of things is abundantly evident in history, and that it will continue to be so hereafter is but too apparent in reason.''[4]

In addition, Locke asserts that, ''if a long train of abuses, prevarications, and artifices, all tending the same way, make the design visible to the people, and they cannot but feel what they lie under, and see whither they are going,[5] ...the people have a right to resist and defend themselves from injury.''[6]

(If some of Locke's passages seem familiar, and they should, it is because Jefferson drew much of his knowledge for the Declaration of Independence from Locke's works.)

To continue, in *Concerning Civil Government*, Locke writes, ''Whenever the legislators endeavor to take away and destroy the property of the people, or to reduce them to slavery under arbitrary power, they put themselves into a state of war with the people, who are thereupon absolved from any further obedience....[And] by this breach of trust they forfeit the power the people had put into their hands for quite contrary ends, and it devolves to the people who have a right to resume their original liberty, and by the establishment of a new legislative..., [to] provide for their own safety and security, which is the end for which they are in society.''[7]

This is the type of reasoning that prompted the Founding Fathers to revolt. They knew they were right to overthrow tyranny and to establish their natural rights and liberties. Although the people ''are more disposed to suffer than right themselves by resistance,'' Locke admits, ''The people shall be the judge.'' Since it is so in the case of private men, why should it be otherwise in that of the greatest moment, where the welfare of millions is concerned. In short, it is up to the people to decide their own destiny—slavery or freedom, as rebellions will occur only when the majority feel that their estates, liberties, and lives are in danger.

Rousseau adds three pertinent thoughts to the discussion: One, since government did not begin with arbitrary power, tyranny is a perversion of lawful government; two, government is completely dissolved by despotism; and three, once accustomed to masters, people are not in a condition to do without them, thus re-emphasizing the importance of maintaining freedom and the ideals of self-government.

Furthermore, Hamilton, in *The Federalist*, No. 28, claims that "If the representatives of the people betray their constituents, there is then no resource left but in the exertion of that original right of self-defense...."

All this discussion on the right to revolt may seem tedious to the reader, but it is imperative that so great an undertaking as a revolution be firmly grounded on sound principles. The American Revolution certainly was.

Now let us analyze the American Revolution to discover its greatness and how to recapture that glory that is our birthright. We shall also briefly study the causes for the failure of the French Revolution.

According to Webster's dictionary, a rebellion is an "open opposition to lawful authority; revolt." But revolution is defined as an "Overthrow of one government, and founding of another; fundamental change in political or social conditions."

Dr. Hannah Arendt further defines a rebellion as a spirit of desperation; a sociological more than a political event. Whereas, a revolution is a political phenomenon; it aims to revise and reorder the current political structure of a society and to do it in a spirit of sobriety and calm rationalness. She considers the French and Russian revolutions more properly as rebellions. The American Revolution led and fought by self-disciplined individuals, was a reluctant, but successful revolution.[8]

Murray N. Rothbard, author of *Conceived in Liberty*, has made one of the most, if not the most, extensive and conclusive studies of American history dating back to the Old World and the subsequent birth of the United States of America. His research and conclusions regarding the American Revolution shed new and brilliant light on America's struggle for freedom and independence.

In Volume I, Dr. Rothbard discusses the characteristics of revolutions: Revolutions are mighty upheavals made by a mass of people, who are willing to rupture the settled habits of a lifetime, including the habit of obedience to an existing government. They are made by people willing to turn from the safe and narrow pursuits of their daily lives to battle violently together in a more general cause. For masses of men to take such a risk requires an accumulation of significant grievances and tensions. No revolution begins in a day and on arbitrary whim. The grievances of the people against their government must pile up and accumulate. Afterward, if held in esteem and cherished, the revolution will decrease the awe in which the government is held and will increase the chances for later revolts against tyranny, if they become necessary.[9]

In Volume III, Dr. Rothbard differentiates between defensive violence and offensive or aggressive violence. He says that violence committed by the people against their oppressors "is a casting off of the unwanted" ruling clique. It is, therefore, "in essence defensive." On the other hand, violence against the people by the government to stem the rising tide of indignation or rebellion by the people and to force the acceptance of an unwanted rule, "is offensive or aggressive....."[10] So there is a crucial difference as to why the government and the people use force: one to subdue free people, the other to reinstate freedom. One is might over right, the other, right over might. This is the essence of the American Revolution, and why it succeeded.

By the same token, Bernard Bailyn, author of *The Ideological Origins of the American Revolution*, shows that the primary goal of the American Revolution was not to overthrow the social order, but to *preserve* the individual rights and liberties that were threatened by corruption of the existing social order. He points out that there were extensive writings before, during, and after the Revolution, often quoting Sidney, Locke, and *Cato*. Over 400 pamphlets, averaging 5,000 to 25,000 words, 10-15 pages in length, were written. They revealed positions taken and the reasons why they were taken—their motives and understanding.[11] Nothing was left to chance.

Later, in 1815, John Adams in a letter to Jefferson asked, "What do we mean by the Revolution? The war? That was no part of the Revolution; it was only an effect and consequence of it. *The Revolution was in the minds of the people*, and this was effected, from 1760 to 1775, in the course of fifteen years before a drop of blood was shed at Lexington. The records of thirteen legislatures, the pamphlets, newspapers in all the colonies, ought to be consulted during that period to ascertain the steps by which the public opinion was enlightened and informed concerning the authority of Parliament over the colonies." (Emphasis added.)

An example of one of the excellent publications of that era was the "Farmer's Letters." Written by John Dickinson, who published a series of twelve weekly letters beginning the week of December 2, 1767; they were mostly directed against the Townshend Act.

The first Letter made the colonists aware of the first political maxim: To divide and conquer. The third exclaimed that the colonists were "ignorant that usurpations, which might have been successfully opposed at first, acquire strength by continuance...." The fifth claimed that Britain should be happy to settle for the increase in trade from her colonies, instead of taxing away incentives. The sixth claimed there was no difference between "internal" and "external" taxes. Both, Dickinson said, were unconstitutional. The seventh and eighth Letters explained that the Townshend Act was enacted merely to set a precedent for the future and that taxes would continue to increase. The ninth warned against the dangers of Britain paying the salaries of judges, governors, and legislatures, which the colonists had been previously paying. The tenth pointed to Ireland as an example of British injustice: After a permanent revenue had been established for the Crown, the revenue went directly to support a horde of British pensioners and holders of sinecure offices, not to the benefit of the people of Ireland. "Some persons," said Dickinson, "may imagine the sums to be raised by the Townshend Act are but small, and therefore may be inclined to acquiesce under it. A conduct more dangerous to freedom, as before has been observed, can never be adopted. Nothing is wanted at home but a *precedent*, the force of which shall be established by the tacit submission of the colonists." The eleventh showed how in England seemingly innocent "precedents had been used as a basis for extremely oppressive measures." And finally, the twelfth Letter summarized the preceding eleven Letters.[12] Consequently, the "Farmer's Letters" became a kind of colonial Bill of Rights.

By 1774, such writings were commonplace. George Washington, writing to Bryan Fairfax on July 20 and August 24, 1774, remarked, "[When] I observe that [the British] government is pursuing a regular plan, at the expense of law and justice, to over-throw our constitutional rights and liberties, how can I expect any redress from a measure which has been ineffectually tried already?...I could wish, I own, that the dispute had been left to posterity to determine, but the crisis is arrived when we must assert our rights or submit to every imposition that can be heaped upon us, till custom and use shall make us...slaves...."[13]

Another example is that of James Otis, who realized the extent of British extravagance when it came to government, bureaucracies, and bureaucrats: "If places, pensions and dependencies shall be ever increased in proportion to new resources, the game may truly be infinite."[14] Thus, the colonists felt it was better to act sooner than later, before such oppressions became entrenched.

The purpose of presenting these writings is to point out how well educated the colonists were in fundamental principles. They had security, position, and wealth, but they valued liberty more. They knew that without liberty there would be no security, no wealth, and no happiness.

Ideas and motives were constantly questioned during the Revolution. Paine said, "The moral principle of revolutions is to instruct, not to destroy," which he helped bring about by his prolific writings. "It is at all times necessary," he added, "and more particularly so during the progress of a revolution, and until right ideas confirm themselves by habit, that we frequently refresh our patriotism by reference to first principles. It is by tracing things to their origin that we learn to understand them: and it is by keeping that line and that origin always in view that we never forget them."

The colonists knew that they were right to fight. They had studied their subject matter well. They were well versed in history, philosophy, and the natural rights of man. They quoted Locke often. They knew Sidney's reasons why everyone might legitimately slay a tyrant; and that a revolution was not an evil, but the greatest weapon for overthrowing tyranny the people had. They knew that there was nothing sacred about governments, and that they ought to be changed as required. Jefferson, too, believed "The spirit of resistance to government is so valuable on certain occasions, that I wish it to be always kept alive." And he knew that injustices made a government illegal.

Likewise, *Cato's Letters* added fuel to the fire. It took Locke's theoretical works and translated them into every day problems for the people to understand. *Cato* wrote, when a government official "exceeds his commission, his acts are as extrajudicial as are those of any private officer usurping an unlawful authority; that is, they are void; and every man is answerable for the wrong which he does. A power to do good can never become a warrant for doing evil." *Cato* also pointed to the corruption and the increasing power of government and its bureaucracy already established in England. These three great writers—Locke, Sidney, and *Cato*—formed a foundation upon which the American Revolution had to succeed.

Furthermore, some of religion's representatives preached against tyranny in favor of natural rights. Jonathan Mayhew, for instance, a deist and Unitarian, delivered what is called the "warning gun of the American Revolution" in *1750*. He proclaimed that "citizens have the right to disobey 'unlawful' authority, [and] in cases of very great and general oppression...to vindicate their natural and legal rights, to break the yoke of tyranny, and free themselves and posterity from inglorious servitude and ruin." The Reverend Samuel Davies, leader of the Southern New Side Presbyterians, declared that the people had a "legal as well as natural right to follow their own judgment." In 1749, the Separates of Canterbury asserted that God's law strictly limited the functions of government to "defense of everyone in the free enjoyment and improvement of life, liberty and property from the force, violence and fraud of others."[15] When they went to do battle, the colonists were well armed—physically and spiritually!

To digress a moment, Rothbard makes an astounding observation that only an armed people's militia could be relied upon to deal successfully with the enemy. In other words, when the cry was sounded, "To arm! To arms! Turn out with your guns!", an unarmed populace would have had no choice but to submit and surrender; there would have been no glorious American Revolution for liberty and freedom. But as history proves, tens of thousands of patriots turned out, ready and *armed* for battle, for which we should be eternally grateful.

Samuel Williams, author of "A Discourse on the Love of Our Country," in 1775 wrote that no one could conceive of America as the cause of a mob, of a party, or a faction. America was the cause of eternal self-defense and liberty.

After the war there was much reflection on its accomplishments. Martin Luther in 1787 summarized the essence of the Revolution: "By the principles of the American Revolution, arbitrary power may, and ought to be resisted even by arms, if necessary."[16]

The reason behind the Revolution quickly spread from a struggle to regain economic liberties into a full-fledged war against all types of tyranny. In fact, contrary to popular opinion that revolutions are led by a few men, this Revolution was endorsed and supported by the majority of the people. For example, in 1774 after the Port of Boston was closed to trade by General Gage, a flock of over 200 sheep were sent to Boston from Windham, Connecticut, accompanied by this letter: "This Town is very sensible of the obligations we, and with us, all British America, are under to the Town of Boston who...are the generous defenders of our common rights and liberties.... And rest assured that if Parliament does not soon afford you relief, and there should in future be any need of our assistance, we shall, with the utmost cheerfulness, exert our influence to that purpose."[17] By the day of Lexington and Concord all thirteen colonies were helping to feed and clothe the people of Boston by gifts of provisions or money or both. Note the benevolent attitude of the colonists; nowhere is it witnessed in subsequent revolutions.

Irving Kristol's lecture "The American Revolution As A Successful Revolution" enumerates the reasons why the Revolution was a success. First, the leaders were able in later years to look with tranquility at what they had produced and they judged it good. Second, this Revolution, unlike all subsequent ones, did not devour its children—the leaders went on to create a new political order, to hold the highest elected offices, and to die peaceful deaths. Third, the feeling of "the revolution betrayed" was absent. Fourth, it was relatively bloodless; the rules of civilized warfare were scrupulously observed; none of the modern-day butchery took place. Fifth, there was no reign of terror, not a single Tory was executed for harboring counter-revolutionary opinions.[18]

Kristol says the American Revolution was so successful that few people nowadays give it serious thought; it is taken for granted. Indeed, soon after it few people gave it serious thought; that is why we have trouble explaining it to ourselves and the world. Since our liberties were obtained, the attention of thinking men has turned away from politics, "so that political theory lost its vigor." Americans cannot articulate the whys and wherefores of the American Revolution. They are losing touch with its greatness, essence, and lesson.

We can thank Dr. Rothbard for his enlightening analysis of the Revolution. The ideology and motivation of the Revolutionary movement, he asserts, was essentially libertarian in thought. There was "no dichotomy between personal and economic freedom, between rights to liberty and to property. These artificial distinctions were left for later ages to construct.... They saw no dichotomy between liberty and economic rights...."[19]

The American Revolution teaches us that the power of government stands ever ready to conspire to violate our liberties; and to stop this crippling and destructive invasion by government, the people must be ever wary, ever vigilant, and ever alert to the conspiracies of their government to expand its power and oppress its citizens. Thus, in the deepest sense, the Revolution was a conscious majority revolution on the side of individual freedom opposed to governmental power. Its ideology was libertarian, stressing the indivisible rights of "Liberty and Property."

Before concluding this chapter, a brief look at the French Revolution may be instructive. At the outset of the French Revolution most Americans wanted to support it, as the French had supported the Americans. But men like Jefferson and Adams considered the French too "depraved" to undertake an experiment in self-government. Even the Frenchman de Tocqueville asserted that it was unbelievable that a liberal, wise, and energetic government could spring from the suffrages of a subservient people. He was right, of course; the French Revolution was a horrendous failure. De Tocqueville concluded that after many years and many governments the French had proved that they were incapable and unworthy of living in freedom.

Why did the French Revolution fail? It was simply a matter of economics. More to the point, the French, after generations of poverty and over-taxation to support spendthrift kings, had just experienced a runaway inflation. There was no gold or silver money with which to trade, and all business was halted. The people were virtually dying of starvation while the government enjoyed prosperity. The French were also spurred on by the success of the American Revolution. So as poor as they were, which was about as poor as possible, the French felt they had nothing to lose and everything to gain by revolting. It was an act of desperation.

The French thought that they would carry the principles of the American Revolution—life, liberty and pursuit of happiness (property)—one step further. They adopted the slogan (and the values) of "liberty, equality and fraternity." With all good intentions and innocence, the French *started* an economic (versus political) revolution in 1789. Sixty years and seven great revolutions later, France was still revolting.

Someone once asked Lafayette what he did during the French Revolution; he answered: "I survived." That, in itself, proved to be an accomplishment.

Here is the crux of the error of the French Revolution. The poor French were led to believe that the property of the wealthy was in some way the result of a theft committed against themselves. They felt that their common wretchedness was due to the laws; thus poverty could be abolished by changing the laws, the system of society. With much envy and resentment among the suffering masses of Paris, these ideas fell on fertile minds.

Still revolting by the mid-1800s, these views, which we call Socialist by today's standards, had reached their economic extreme. Abolish inequality of fortunes, of education, and of the sexes, the French cried. They demanded remedies for poverty and against the disease called work. Finally, workmen carried weapons and demanded pay for no work—landlords should give rooms rent-free!

After each revolution the people thought it was the last, and they believed it. But the Revolution's "work" dragged on through seven major revolutions: 1) The ancient Regime (pre-1789), 2) Constitutional Monarchy, 3) Republic, 4) Empire (Napoleon), 5) Restoration, 6) July Monarchy, and 7) the February Revolution of 1848.

The French Revolution became a "class struggle" based on Socialist ideas. Therefore, it was doomed to fail from the start. And this bloody, revengeful, despairing type of revolution became the model for all subsequent revolutions. Consequently, all future revolutions—the Russian, Mexican, South American, Spanish, Chinese, and African—have failed, too.

Americans realized that wealth is a result of freedom and production. Poverty can only be eliminated by work. The French believed, as do all socialists, that wealth can be redistributed, thus eliminating poverty. The American Revolution promised freedom in which to work and in which to pursue one's happiness. The French Revolution promised to abolish poverty, as all revolutions since have promised. Instead of realizing that poverty is abolished by economic growth, not by economic redistribution (for there is never enough to redistribute), the French only succeeded in creating violent rebellions which, in turn, created more instability, uncertainty, and poverty, leading to further rebellions.

The American Revolution set a splendid example for the world. Perhaps if the French Revolution had not followed the American so closely and had not been so "exciting" and drawn-out, the world would better remember the American Revolution. However, the example of the American Revolution still stands and we would do well to heed it: Security and property are a result of, and an effect of, freedom and liberty. There cannot be security and wealth where there is no freedom. Freedom is the ultimate, the crucial value for which to fight. That is what the American Revolution was all about; and that is what any future revolutions ought to be about.

"They accomplished a revolution which has no parallel in the annals of human society," remarked Madison in No. 14 of *The Federalist*. And they did it because Americans "are warranted by the laws of God and nature, in the use of every rightful act and energy of *policy, stratagem,* and *force*" to so secure their rights and liberties. So wrote the town of Pembroke, Massachusetts around late 1772.

The phenomenal effect of the American Revolution has been best described by Paine. In the introduction of the second part of his *Rights of Man*, written February 17, 1792, Paine says: "What Archimedes said of the mechanical powers, may be applied to reason and liberty: 'Had we,' said he, 'a place to stand upon, we might raise the world.' The Revolution of America presented in politics what was only theory in mechanics. So deeply rooted were all the governments of the old world, and so effectually had the tyranny and the antiquity of habit established itself over the mind, that no beginning could be made in Asia, Africa, or Europe, to reform the political condition of man. Freedom had been hunted round the globe; reason was considered as rebellion; and the slavery of fear had made man afraid to think. But such is the irresistable nature of truth, that all it asks, and all it wants, is the liberty of appearing...and no sooner did the American governments display themselves to the world, than despotism felt a shock, and man began to contemplate redress."

NOTES ON REVOLUTION, CHAPTER VI

1. Op. Cit., P. 706.
2. Op. Cit., P. 431.
3. *Great Books*, Volume 3, A Syntopicon II, P. 632.
4. Op. Cit., Pp. 20-21.
5. IBID., P. 77.
6. IBID., P. 79.
7. IBID., P. 76.
8. Irving Kristol speech, October 12, 1973, "The American Revolution as A Successful Revolution," P. 8.
9. (New Rochelle, New York: Arlington House, 1975), Volume I, Pp. 103-05.
10. IBID., P. 197.
11. (Cambridge, Mass.: The Belknap Press of Harvard University Press, 1967), P. vi.
12. Bernhard Knollenberg, *Growth of the American Revolution 1766-1775*, (New York: The Free Press, 1975), Pp. 49-53.
13. IBID., P. 132.
14. IBID., P. 133.
15. *Conceived in Liberty*, Volume II, Pp. 196-97.
16. *Annals of America*, Volume 3, P. 166.
17. *Growth of American Revolution*, P. 164.
18. Op. Cit., Pp. 6-7.
19. *Conceived in Liberty*, Volume III, P. 351.

VII

Constitution

All human constitutions are subject to corruption, and must perish unless they are timely renewed, and reduced to their first principles.
ALGERNON SIDNEY

Constitutions usually follow revolutions; thus, this chapter is about the United States Constitution, what it means, how it has been corrupted, and how to return its spirit to first principles. In Paine's work "On Constitutions" he defines a constitution not as an act of a government, but of a people constituting government. The constitution is not only an authorization for government authority, but also a control on government power.

In 1791, President Washington requested Jefferson to submit his opinion regarding the proposal to adopt a national bank. The bulk of Jefferson's argument against adoption of the plan rested on it being unconstitutional. His proof was the Tenth Amendment, which reads: "The powers not delegated to the United States by the Constitution, nor prohibited by it to the States, are reserved to the States respectively or to the people." He added, "To take a single step beyond the boundaries thus specially drawn around the powers of Congress is to take possession of a boundless field of power, *no longer susceptible of any definition*." (Emphasis added.)

To stay within the literal meaning of the Constitution is what is meant by "strict construction" of it. Jefferson's reasoning is the best reason why the Constitution should be held to the strict meaning of every word. In *The Federalist*, No. 78, Hamilton wrote that no legislative act contrary to the Constitution can be valid. To deny this would be to affirm that the deputy is greater than his principal; that men acting by virtue of powers may do not only what their powers do not authorize, but what they forbid. A constitution, is in fact, a fundamental law. Whenever a particular statute contravenes the Constitution, it is the duty of the judiciary to strike it down.

The aforementioned is simple justice. After all, there is no reason to go to the trouble of preparing a constitution if it is not honored and respected. To ignore or disregard its literal meaning is not only unjust, but will lead to other usurpations as well.

Some of the great Founding Fathers opposed the adoption of the Constitution. Their arguments are useful today because they point out the weaknesses of the Constitution. They show how injustices are committed today under the protection of the Constitution, but in the name of justice.

The Anti-Federalists by Jackson Turner Main, enumerates the chief objections to ratification of the Constitution. The Anti-Federalists accused the Constitutional Convention of going beyond its delegated power and purpose. It violated its instruction and acted illegally. Its sole and express purpose was merely to revise the Articles of Confederation. Therefore, the first objection was that the Constitution was a large move away from the Articles of Confederation. The compact between the States was radically changed to a national government, leaving the States with but a shadow of their former power.

Second, they objected to a national government being given the power to tax and to raise an army. Formerly, Congress had no taxing power and the States protected themselves with their own militia. These new powers over the "purse and the sword" were considered extremely dangerous.

Another objection was the use of broad grants of power and the use of ambiguous terms such as the "general welfare," the "necessary and proper," and the "supreme law of the land" clauses. Very few individuals, it was argued, would understand the Constitution, leaving Congress to be its own interpreter. And Congress could interpret the Constitution with the most ambitious and arbitrary purposes in mind. In addition, the Constitution failed to reserve any powers to the States.

Fourth, by forming a national government, the Constitutional Convention violated history's lesson that freedom could be maintained only by local governments. The less local a government is, the more likely it is to become oppressive.

Fifth, since it appeared that the Convention gave nearly all the important powers to Congress, John Quincy Adams figured that the rich would become richer and the Constitution "would bring free government to an end."[1]

One thing is certain, the Anti-Federalists did not worry in vain.

There was much literature written in opposition to the Constitution, and surprisingly little of it has reached our history text books. One of the most penetrating thinkers of that era was Patrick Henry. He understood the nature of the new government more thoroughly and foresaw its practical workings more clearly than most of his contemporaries.

His first objection was: "Who authorized them (the framers) to speak the language of, *we the people*, instead of *we the States*?"

Then he went on to object to numerous defects in the Constitution. Out of twenty-two days of debate in the Virginia convention for ratification, Henry spoke against ratification on seventeen days. In one speech he was on his feet for seven hours. Another speech occupies forty pages in the Convention's journal. He fought for a bill of rights of twenty amendments. It is too bad only ten were adopted. As Professor Hare, a writer on constitutional law, opined, "The restraints [on government] should therefore be so explicit that they cannot be misunderstood."[2]

Henry predicted that if the Constitution were to be adopted government expenses would increase tenfold, a numerous standing army would be established, and finally there would be a long and rapacious train of officers and dependents whose compensations would be without limitation.[3] He foretold that the federal government would oppress the States using a "standing army to execute the execrable commands of tyranny." In other words, Henry realized that "State's Rights" had been abolished and prophecied the physical result of that contradiction in a civil war.

In writing to Richard Henry Lee, he warned of despotic power in the executive: "For Rights, without having power and might is but a shadow.... See how rapidly power grows, how slowly the means of curbing it. That the president is to be accountable for the general success of government is precisely the principle of every Despotism—because if we look to him for success in every department he must have power over them, and having that power, which is necessary to secure success, he is *ipso facto*, a despot."[4]

"At present we have our liberties and privileges in our hands. Let us not relinquish them," he implored. "Let us not adopt this system till we see them secured." Henry's great objection to this government was, "that it does not leave us the means of defending our rights; or, of waging war against tyrants."[5] He feared that under this Constitution the Federal government would tax and grow strong to the detriment of the States and of the individual citizens.

Another excellent writer who argued against ratification was Richard Henry Lee, also a distinguished and influential representative from Virginia. "The first maxim of a man who loves liberty," he declared, "should be never to grant to rulers an atom of power that is not most clearly and indispensably necessary for the safety and well being of society." He was convinced the new government would pave the way to an "elective despotism."

Lee feared that the consolidation of the states could not happen easily, that it would eventually result in "convulsions and civil wars." He added, "Whether such a change will not totally destroy the liberties of this country, time only can determine." He noticed there were deposited in the general government some undefined important powers, which "may be used to good or bad purposes as honest or designing men shall prevail."[6]

Lee understood that thousands of men were ready to adopt the "essentially defective" Constitution. He spoke out about such a "pernicious idea; it argues a servility of character totally unfit for the support of free government; it is very repugnant to that jealousy respecting liberty, so absolutely necessary in all free states...."[7]

He blamed the acceptance of the Constitution on a few designing men who had prepared the people by devious methods. He said the states had been unsettled by making tender, suspension, and paper-money laws. The conduct of several legislatures had prepared many honest men for changes in government, which otherwise they would not have considered.

In Pennsylvania the same accusation was made: "While the gilded chains were [being forged in the Convention], the meaner instruments of the despotism without were busily employed in alarming the fears of the people with dangers which did not exist, and exciting their hopes of greater advantages from the expected plan than even the best government on earth could produce."[8] These invented fears were that foreign invasion was more likely to occur and anarchy would reign if no formal government existed. Such fears were groundless. If one reads the Articles of Confederation, which were still in force at that time, one can only marvel at their simplicity and directness. They were so effective that the thirteen colonies under their aegis fought the War of Independence successfully.

To summarize the argument against ratification, here are the reasons for dissent by the Anti-Federalists of Pennsylvania: Are the people

> "repenting of the folly of so recently asserting their unalienable rights against foreign despots at the expense of so much blood and treasure, [that] the people of America are now willing to resign every privilege of freemen, and submit to the dominion of an absolute government that will embrace all America in one chain of despotism? Or will they, with virtuous indignation, spurn at the shackles prepared for them, and confirm their liberties by a conduct becoming freemen?
>
> That the new government will not be a confederacy of states, as it ought, but one consolidated government, founded upon the destruction of the several governments of the states...
>
> The powers of Congress under the new Constitution are complete and unlimited over the purse and the sword, and are perfectly independent of and supreme over the state governments, whose intervention in these

> great points is entirely destroyed. By virtue of their power of taxation, Congress may command the whole or any part of the property of the people."[9]

This chapter is not to discourage the reader's belief in the efficacy of the Constitution, but to make him aware of the defects in the document so he can be on guard against possible usurpations of his rights. It is all too clear by now that this has been the case all along. Justice, therefore, demands that this kind of despotism be stopped. To condone a "loose construction" of the Constitution is to play into the hands of those who would take away your rights. In any compromise of your rights, you lose.

It becomes easy to see how changes in the government by expansion of its powers has lead to many of today's problems (which are discussed in later chapters). The answer must necessarily lie, therefore, in reinterpreting the literal meaning back into the Constitution. To paraphrase Herbert Spencer: The function of Liberalism in the past was that of putting a limit to the powers of kings. The function of true Liberalism in the future will be that of putting a limit to the powers of Congress.

Sidney laid the blame for allowing rights to be lost and constitutions misinterpreted squarely on the shoulders of the citizens. "Taking our affairs at the worst, we shall soon find, that if we have the same spirit they [the framers] had, we may easily restore our nation to its ancient liberty, dignity, and happiness; and if we do not, the fault is owning to ourselves and not to any want of virtue and wisdom in them."

That responsibility is now on the shoulders of every American. Will the standard for freedom, liberty, and justice be raised before it is too late for America? All we need is the will to change things. We still have the opportunity to seek redress from our representatives. It is up to us to use it!

NOTES ON CONSTITUTION, CHAPTER VII

1. *The Anti-Federalists, Critics of the Constitution 1781-1788*, (New york: W.W. Norton & Co., Inc., 1961), Pp. 120-129,175.
2. William Wirt Henry, *Patrick Henry, Life, Correspondence and Speeches*, (New York: Charles Scribner's Sons, 1891), Volume II, Chapter 37.
3. *Annals of America*, Volume 3, P. 282.
4. *Patrick Henry*, Volume III.
5. IBID.
6. *Annals of America*, Volume 3, Pp. 130-133.
7. IBID., P. 136.
8. IBID., P. 173.
9. IBID., P. 177.

VIII

Law

A good tree brings forth good fruit by nature, without compulsion; is it not madness to prescribe laws to an apple-tree that it shall bear apples and not thorns?
LUTHER

Of all the topics covered in this book, none is so popular as Law. Nearly all writers of esteem have had something to say on the subject. They have also had something to say about legislators and precedents, both of which will be included in this chapter.

Laws are important because they are the official rules of society—the rules of the game by which everyone plays. They establish the extent to which we live by justice or injustice. As they implement the Constitution, the supreme law of the land, they either protect or violate our individual rights. Thus, they are a crucial part of society and of this book.

One of the greatest lawgivers of all time was Solon, who lived between 638-539 B.C., before both Plato and Aristotle. Since men keep their promises when neither side can get anything by the breaking of them, Solon, Plutarch tells us, "would so fit his laws to the citizens, that all should understand it was more eligible to be just than to break the laws."[1]

Aristotle says that in all sciences and arts the end is good; in political science the good is justice.[2] Regarding lawgivers, he reflected on how strange it was that the statesman should always be considering how he can dominate and tyrannize over others, whether he will or not. How can that which is not even lawful be the business of the statesmen or legislator, he queried. For it is certainly not lawful to rule without regard to justice, for there may be might where there is no right. The other arts and sciences offer no parallel; a physician is not expected to persuade or coerce his patients, nor a pilot the passengers in his ship. Yet most men appear to think that the art of despotic government is statesmanship, and what men affirm to be unjust and inexpedient in their own case they are not ashamed of practicing toward others; they demand just rule for themselves, but where other men are concerned they care nothing about it. Such behavior is irrational.[3] Aristotle certainly was observant, for who else goes into business and forces his customers to abide by his wishes, but the legislator.

To speak of two different types of law is Aristotle's next subject in *Rhetoric*. There is particular law, which each community lays down and applies to its own members, and universal law, which is the law of Nature. For there really is, as every one to some extent divines, a natural justice and injustice that is binding on all men.[4]

Aristotle concludes his thoughts on law with a surprising statement: "We do not regard ourselves as bound to observe a bad law which it was a mistake ever to pass."[5] It is no wonder that Aristotle is called the father of mankind. He laid the foundation for law squarely on top of justice, for all future generations to practice.

To expand further on laws, Hobbes in his *Leviathan*, opens with the fact that civil and natural laws are different but equal parts of law; one part, being written, is called *civil*, the other unwritten, *natural*; and no law can ever be against reason.[6]

Then Hobbes divides laws into natural and positive, and under positive, into distributive and penal. Laws which are natural are those which have been laws from all eternity, and are called not only natural, but also *moral* laws, consisting of the moral virtues, such as justice and equity. Positive are those which have been made laws by the sovereign power. Distributive are those that determine the rights of the subjects, declaring to every man what is his. And penal are those which declare what penalty shall be inflicted on those that violate the law.[7] In this context it is easy to understand the purpose of law. It is easier to judge which laws are good and bad, right and wrong, just and unjust.

Regarding precedents, Hobbes declares that men's judgments have been perverted by trusting to them. For example, he says, though the sentence of the judge be a law to the party pleading, it is no law to any judge that shall succeed him in that office. For a judge may err in the interpretation even of written laws; but no error of a subordinate judge can change the law.

"The public good is the rule and measure of all lawmaking," says Locke. He adds that the legislature cannot transfer the power of making laws to any other hands,[8] so as to preclude the executive and judicial branches from making laws by using executive orders and precedents. For the people delegated that power to their legislators only.

Locke observed that because those laws which are constantly to be in effect may be made in a little time, there is no need for the legislature to be always in session. Of course, that would put an end to most of today's proliferation of laws that legislators think they are hired to pass. For once the general rules of society are made, it is up to everyone to run his own life as he sees fit, without continual interference and coercion from new and complicated laws.

This leads us to the conclusion that too many laws may destroy the very reason for laws in the first place. A minimum of just and objective laws are necessary to liberty. But too many laws would cause property rights to become uncertain. The citizens would lose their liberty and security.

Cato's Letters (No. 99), suggests that legislators are elected to protect the people's liberty. Thus, honor, virtue and conscience should be as active as falsehood, corruption, injustice, barbarism, and treachery. Otherwise, government descends from a blessing to a burden. For as Sidney wrote, "Laws were made to direct and instruct magistrates, and, if they will not be directed, to restrain them." He also agrees with Aristotle that that which is not just is not law; and that which is not law, ought not to be obeyed.

So far the best standard by which to judge laws comes from Adam Smith's *The Wealth of Nations*. Written over 200 years ago it contains the essence of the idea of a free society: the law ought always to trust people with the care of their own lives, as in their own situations they must be able to judge better of it than the legislators can do.[9] But, of course, we have had a hard time convincing legislators to see it that way.

Montaigne, for instance, complained back in the 1500s that: "The worst thing I find in our state is instability, and that our laws, no more than our clothes, cannot settle in any certain form."[10]

Besides being just, simple and few, laws, to be a rule of action, must be known, permanent and stable. Since the law is the measure of civil right, it must be unchanging or the thing measured never can be settled. How else can property be secure? It must keep guilt and innocence apart by a distinct and definite limitation. Deviations from the law must be uniformly punished, or no man can be certain when he shall be safe.[11]

The next section of writing is representative of the American Revolutionary era. Sam Adams, the fire-brand of the Revolution, noted that all positive and civil laws should conform, as far as possible, to the law of natural reason and equity. On the subject of legislators he remarked, "As the first fundamental natural law is the preservation of society, legislatures have no right to absolute, arbitrary power over the lives and fortunes of the people. They are therefore, bound to see that justice is dispensed."

Richard Henry Lee wrote that a free people ought to form their government and laws so as to create a confidence in and respect for them, thus earning the support of the community.

A fundamentalist, Paine simple stated, "That which is law for the individual, is likewise law for the state." In other words, the state is not bigger or more important than the individual and cannot, therefore, oppress him under such laws as those of eminent domain or those for the good of society or those for the general welfare.

Regarding precedents, Paine spoke very strongly against their usage. He warned that "Government by precedent, without any regard to the principle of the precedent, is one of the vilest systems that can be set up. In numerous instances, the precedent ought to operate as a warning, and not as an example, and requires to be shunned instead of imitated...."[12] Furthermore, he argued that every case ought to be determined on its own merits, without the farce of what are called precedents. In courts of arbitration, justice and good judgment should preside. It is the mark of barbarians to obey precedents.

Jonathan Swift also stated what he thought of lawyers and precedents in no uncertain terms: "It is a maxim among these men [lawyers], that whatever has been done before, may legally be done again, and therefore they take special care to record all the decisions formerly made, even those which have, through ignorance or corruption, contradicted the rules of common justice, and the general reason of mankind. These under the name of *precedents*, they produce as authorities, and thereby endeavor to justify the most iniquitous opinions...."[13]

It seems that all learned individuals consider the use of precedents as the mark of barbarians. In fact, lawyers were so unpopular around the 1780s, there was a movement to abolish the profession. For the "rapacity of lawyers was regarded as contributing to the general distress."[14] Even Mr. Gallatin, American Minister in France and England, in 1831 said that "Without the lawyers we should by now have revised our civil law, but they defend the abuses and ambiguities from which they profit." To compound the problem, nine out of ten Congressmen were lawyers, de Tocqueville noticed.

Since Jefferson wrote on nearly every topic imaginable, it is not surprising to find that he wrote on legislatures. At the age of 74, in a letter to Francis Walker Gilmer, dated June 7, 1816, Jefferson declared, "Our legislators are not sufficiently apprised of the rightful limits of their powers, that their true office is to declare and enforce only our natural rights and duties, and to take none of them from us." If they actually did this, it would lessen their labor and lighten equally our municipal codes. Jefferson worried when he saw legislators keeping themselves too busy. He believed that "the path we have to pursue is so quiet that we have nothing scarcely to propose to our Legislature. A noiseless course, not meddling with the affairs of others, unattentive of notice, is a mark that society is going on in happiness." We can only construe then that our busybody legislature of today is up to no good.

One of the best works on the topic of law is Frederic Bastiat's *The Law*. First published in 1850, it is still in print today as one of the finest discourses on the relationship between law and liberty. Bastiat was a French economist, statesman, and author. He defined law as "the collective organization of the individual right to lawful defense."

Each of us has a natural right to defend his person, his liberty, and his property, he declared. These are the three basic requirements of life, and the preservation of any one of them is completely dependent upon the preservation of the other two. Since an individual cannot *lawfully* use force against the person, liberty, or property of another individual, then the common force—the law—for the same reason, cannot *lawfully* be used to destroy the person, liberty, or property of individuals or groups. This is a perversion of force. The law is merely an organization of the natural right of lawful defense. It is the substitution of a common force for individual forces. And this common force ought to do only what the individual forces have a natural and lawful right to do: to protect life and property, causing justice to reign over all of us.[15] In short, law is organized to further justice; it is organized to act as an obstacle to injustice.

In the chapter on justice we established the fact that justice exists with or without and before law. Therefore, to proclaim that all good and bad stems from law is to reverse cause and effect and can only lead to disastrous consequences. For example, to make the law responsible for individual misfortunes, social inequalities, and economic differences, is to open the door to an endless succession of complaints, irritations, troubles, and revolutions. After all, the law is, by definition, *justice*!

When the law is used for things other than justice, there is no end to the misery created. Here are some of the examples of the problems created by legislative interference, as cited by the British libertarian Herbert Spencer, in his *The Man Versus The State*. The first point Spencer makes is that the legislator thinks his laws will stop where he intends them to stop. One of the numerous examples Spencer uses is that of legislators, who in 1833 voted 30,000 pounds a year to aid in building schoolhouses, never suspecting that the step they took would lead to forced contributions, local and general, amounting to 10,000,000 pounds by 1890; "they did not intend to establish the principle that A should be made responsible for educating B's offspring," but that is what happened.[16]

Another example is that of the Mercantile Marine Act. "The examinations devised for insuring the efficiency of captains have had the effect of certifying the superficially clever and unpractised men, and, as we are told by a shipowner, rejecting many of the long-tried and most trustworthy: the general result being that *the ratio of shipwrecks has increased*."[17]

The question that legislators should be asking themselves is, "What type of social structure am I tending to produce?" But that is a question they never entertain. The more numerous governmental interventions become, the more confirmed do their habits grow, the reason being that more laws seem necessary to supplement the first ineffective measures, and for dealing with artificially caused evils.

Spencer points out that nowhere is there so astounding a contrast between the difficulty of the task and the unpreparedness of the persons who undertake it as there is in lawmaking. One of the most monstrous beliefs is that while for a simple handicraft, such as shoemaking, a long apprenticeship is needful, the making of a nation's laws requires no apprenticeship at all!

Spencer suggests that legislators should be held responsible for their actions, that he who helps to pass a law, can no more be absolved if misery and mortality result from it than the journeyman druggist can be absolved when death is caused by the medicine he ignorantly prescribes.[18] This idea has certain possibilities. What would happen to all the "do-good" legislation, if legislators were held accountable for their actions? If it were proven, for example, that drug legislation has actually created the drug culture instead of eliminated it, maybe then the maxim "quality rather than quantity" would again mean something to "practical" politicians.

The final point Spencer makes is on the subject of the misplaced "worship of the legislature." He says a change of feeling comes over constituencies when their members pass in to the Legislative Chamber. As soon as they assemble at Westminster, charges of the incompetence and folly, that had been showered on them from press to platform, cease and unlimited faith emerges. All of a sudden there is nothing which the elected legislator's "newly acquired" wisdom and power cannot accomplish.

To sum up so far, we have just read how the ancient Greeks thought that law was based on justice and reason. Later on, laws were passed to protect individual rights, but too many laws destroy those very same rights, so too many laws bring about perversion of the law. We read that the use of precedents was evil and unjust. And finally we came to the point that unskilled legislators bring about disastrous consequences. Yet voters seem to see elected officials as saviors of a sort of mankind, in whom they place unlimited faith and patience. If law does not once again become predicated on justice, instead of good intentions, then injustice, injuries, and revolutions can only be the consequences.

The reader may ask how the law gets perverted since justice seems so simple to understand. Mencken illustrates one way the law gets turned around. He says that as a child he was taught that the aim of the Bill of Rights and Constitution was to keep lawmakers from running amok. But by the 1930s the prevailing beliefs were that "the law-making bodies should be free to experiment almost *ad libitum*... and that it is the chief business of the Supreme Court to keep the Constitution loose and elastic, so that blasting holes through it may not be too onerous."

That is precisely what Congress did: During the 1930s massive volumes of legislation flowed through Congress, creating disruptions throughout the country, most of which still haunt us today and help to explain why more and more laws seem to be called for (to solve the original government-created problems).

When Congress abdicated its responsibility and chose instead to whitewash the country's problems with coatings of obnoxious laws, it disintegrated into a creature at the mercy of pressure groups, of dubious wisdom and even more dubious honesty. Laws were no longer made by a rational process of public discussion; they were made by a process of blackmail and intimidation (and were executed in the same manner). The typical lawmaker nowadays, claimed Mencken, is a man wholly devoid of principle—a mere puppet in a grotesque game. If the right pressure could be applied to him he would be cheerfully in favor of polygamy, astrology or cannibalism.[19] And that, dear reader, was the state of affairs of our Legislature fifty years ago!

In a more serious vein, there is a very ominous and dangerous result of too many laws. For instance, a prodigous amount of laws leads to an increased amount of lawbreaking, and, in turn, to growing law enforcement agencies, which lead to larger government. It is definitely a case of government perpetuating itself. Perhaps it really wants the law broken! Such a wish could be construed as a flagrant grab for power.

For there is no other way to rule innocent men. The power any government has is the power to crack down on criminals. When there are not enough criminals, a government *makes* them, simply by declaring so many things to be a crime that it becomes impossible for men to live without breaking laws. A nation of law-abiding citizens needs no huge law enforcement system. But pass the kind of laws that can neither be observed, or enforced, or objectively interpreted, and a nation of law-breakers is created. Then government can cash in.[20]

This is the implication of the purpose of creating "victimless crimes," "state crimes," and "social crimes." The advent of biased laws has always been the cause of unrest, wars, and revolutions, governments' favorite exercises.

We have come full circle, from protection of individual rights by law to the destruction of individual rights by law. It is vital to realize that there ought to be no conflict between law and freedom. Thus it is immeasurably more important to preserve the Bill of Rights and the Constitution than it is to pass legislation, however beneficial it may seem at the time. The rule of law requires that all laws conform to certain principles. Hence, laws are *not* to be *created*, but to be *discovered*, as are the laws of Nature. This is the key. This would stop the proliferation of laws in the legislature and change it to a *law-finding* body, to base its business on reason, justice, and freedom.

"True law," said Cicero, "is right reason in agreement with nature;" it is of universal application, unchanging and everlasting as the hills. There ought not to be different laws at different places, nor different laws now and in the future, but one eternal and unchangable law to be valid for all nations and at all times. That is the sum of law and justice.

As we conclude, Locke shows us what the benefits of law should be: The end of law is, not to abolish or restrain, but to preserve and enlarge freedom. For where there is no law there is no freedom. For liberty implies being free from restraint and violence from others; and freedom cannot exist where there is no law: Liberty is to dispose as one wishes, of his person, action, possessions, and his whole property, within the allowance of those laws, and not to be the subject of the arbitrary will of another, but to freely follow his own.

NOTES ON LAW, CHAPTER VIII

1. Op. Cit., P. 66.
2. Op. Cit., P. 480.
3. IBID., Pp. 528-29.
4. IBID., P. 617.
5. IBID., P. 621
6. Op. Cit., Pp. 131-32.
7. IBID., Pp. 136-37.
8. Op. Cit., Pp. 11 and 58.
9. Op. Cit., P. 228.
10. Op. Cit., P. 319.
11. James Boswell, *The Life of Samuel Johnson, LL.D.*, Pp. 204-05.
12. William M. Van der Weyde, *The Life and Works of Thomas Paine*, Patriot's Edition, Introduction by Thomas A. Edison, (New Rochelle, New York: Thomas Paine National Historical Association, 1925) Vol. VI, "Rights of Man," Part Second, Chapter 7.
13. *Conceived in Liberty*, Vol.III, P. 98.
14. *Anti-Federalists*, P. 57.
15. Op. Cit., Pp. 6-7.
16. Op. Cit., P. 29.
17. IBID., P. 132.
18. IBID., P. 120.
19. *The Vintage Mencken*, gathered by Alistair Cooke, (New York: Vintage Books, Various), Pp. 190-92.
20. *Atlas Shrugged*, P. 436.

IX

Republic

At the close of the Constitution Convention, Benjamin Franklin was asked, "What is the kind and form of our government?" He answered, "A Republic—if you can keep it!"

Since the United States is a republic, not a democracy, it is important for the understanding of political justice to know what a republic really is.

The form of our government is republican in nature, i.e., the House of Representatives is elected directly by the people; this is the only concession to democracy. The Senate (prior to the Seventeenth Amendment), was elected by state legislatures. The President is elected by electors, not by direct vote of the people. It was supposed to be a democratic republic, where the people retained the supreme power, exercised through their representatives.

A republican form of government is the hardest to keep because it depends upon self-government, which in turn depends upon independent people. People who prefer security to freedom will lose their republic by default in the process of turning it into a democracy, which promises more benefits, but at the expense of freedom. Jefferson knew how demanding a republic is; even though we did produce a near perfect republic, he wondered whether the people would keep it, or lose the memory of freedom in the enjoyment of plenty. "Material abundance without character is the surest way to destruction."

In *The Federalist*, No. 39, Madison insisted upon a republican form of government, since "no other form would be reconcilable with the genius of the people of America; with the fundamental principles of the Revolution; or with that honorable determination...to rest all our political experiments on the capacity of mankind for self-government."

Jefferson believed in the efficacy of reason and opposed any and all forms of tyranny, either of body or mind. He said, "Sometimes it is said that man cannot be trusted with the government of himself. Can he then be trusted with the government of others? Or have we found angels in the forms of Kings to govern him?" He believed that that form of government is best, which communicates ease, comfort, security, or in one word, happiness, to the greatest number of persons, and in the highest degree; that the happiness and dignity of mankind consist in virtue; and that virtue is the foundation of republican government.

Mill noticed that Americans in the 1800's carried on their business very well with little or no government: "let them be left without a government, every body of Americans is able to improvise one, and to carry on that or any other public business with a sufficient amount of intelligence, order, and decision. This is what every free people ought to be.... But where everything is done through the bureaucracy, nothing to which the bureaucracy is really adverse can be done at all."[1] Therefore, the principle of responsibility secures the greatest good in society.

What this newly created republic was to be was an extremely decentralized national government, where the real power was to be in the hands of people on their local level. As Jefferson conceptualized: "Let the general government be reduced to foreign concerns only.... Our country is too large to have all its affairs directed by a single government...." He warned what would happen if the general government embraced most of the power: It "would become the most corrupt government on the earth.... What an augmentation of the field for jobbing, speculating, plundering, office building, and office hunting would be produced...!" He added, "Let our affairs be disentangled from those of all other nations, except to commerce, which the merchants will manage the better the more they are left free to manage for themselves, and our general government may be reduced to a very simple organization, and a very unexpensive one...."

Jefferson alone achieved this. Upon taking office in 1801 as the third President, he took a meat-ax to government. He cut the size of government in half, abolished all internal taxes, set up a program of paying off the national debt in fifteen years, and had enough money (gold) left to make the Louisiana Purchase for $11,250,000. When his term expired he joyfully looked forward to becoming a private citizen again; he remarked, "I have the consolation too of having added nothing to my private fortune during my public service, and of retiring with hands as clean as they are empty." He was the first and last president to live up to the American ideals of a republican form of government. The point is—it is possible!

Republicanism is the protectorate of minorities, and the consecration of self-government. In an extensive country, it can prevail only by the union of several independent states or communities in a single confederacy. A large republic not founded on the federal principle must result in the government of a single city like Rome or Paris. In other words, a great democracy must either sacrifice self-government to unity, or preserve it by federalism. The multiplication of centers of government promotes the diffusion of political knowledge, power, and healthy and independent opinion.

Our Founding Fathers were aware of this, of course; so they constructed a republican form of government consisting of independent states. In fact, the Constitution, Article 4, Section 4, *guarantees* a republican form of government to every State in the Union. It cannot be too emphasized that republican government is the only form of government which is not eternally at open or secret war with the rights of the people.

Indeed, Jefferson wrote a letter to Joseph C. Cabell, February, 1816, which expounded on the meaning of republicanism. Liberty and the rights of man in every government which has ever existed under the sun has always been destroyed by the generalizing and concentrating of all cares and powers into one body, he noted. The secret of freedom will be the individual "making himself the depository of the powers respecting himself," and delegating fewer and fewer powers as officials become farther removed from him, so that the federal government holds the least amount of power. For is it not absurd to suppose any man or body of men can arbitrarily exercise their wisdom over a statewide or nationwide area with any kind of success, knowing that ordinary men have a very short radius of operation?

Moreover, says Jefferson, "by placing under everyone what his own eye may superintend," there is erected the surest safeguard against usurpation of function. "Where every man is a sharer in the direction of his ward-republic, or some of the higher ones, and feels that he is a participator in the government of affairs, not merely at an election one day in the year, but every day...he will let the heart be torn out of his body sooner than his power wrested from him by a Caesar or a Bonaparte."

The Founding Fathers were well aware of democracy's excesses, its leveling-down process, its inherent seeds of destruction, and of Plato's warning that unrestricted democracy must result in dictatorship. Therefore, the American Republic was to be a constitutional republic with individual liberty, elected representatives, and limited government—in that order. The individual's rights were unalienable, to be protected and guarded by the elected representatives; the government's power was to be delimited and nailed down. The power to govern was checked and balanced by three different branches of the government—the executive, legislative, and judicial. In addition, the individual, the holder of the supreme power, was to be the final and greatest check of all. And in between the general government and the citizen were the state governments, the first line of defense. No despot, no tyrant, not even a majority, were to separate the citizen from his rights.

To insure this process, republican government was to be rigorously frugal and simple, applying all the possible savings of the public revenue to the discharge of the national debt; there were to be no multiplication of officers and salaries merely to make partisans and for increasing, by every devise, the public debt on the onerous principle of its being a public blessing. Such was Jefferson's vision.

Hamilton, too, believed that frugality and economy "become the modest simplicity of republican government." (No. 34, *The Federalist.*)

Upon his return from America, de Tocqueville commented that the United States republic had not been the assailant, but the guardian, of all vested rights; the property of individuals had better guarantees there than in any other country of the world; anarchy there had been as unknown as despotism. But the principles on which the American Constitution rest and sincere respect for right are indispensable to all republics, he said. "And it may be said beforehand that wherever they are not found, the republic will soon have ceased to exist."[2]

Republican government, according to Lord Acton, is also the only method of curbing the power of the majority.

How can every citizen take part in his government? If the federal government held little power, i.e., only in foreign, non-trade affairs, the states, cities and towns would hold the bulk of the power-making decision. And the majority of power would be in one's own neighborhood. This is the way our government was set up.

An excellent small book on why and how to return to neighborhood governments has been written by Milton Kotler, entitled: *Neighborhood Government: The Local Foundations of Political Life.*

Here are presented some of the key ideas of the book. Kotler says modern cities have been growing by annexing local towns and suburbs. The purpose of the modern city "functions on the basis of three principles. One is to monopolize all regional political power in the original city, or downtown," thus rapidly eliminating any competing independent political entity. Second, annexation is used to exploit the wealth of the region until neighborhoods become impoverished, while downtowns become enriched. This can be seen in the consolidation of financial and commercial power downtown. Third, the purpose which annexation serves is to impose on the subjugated political units the burden of paying disproportionately the costs of city administration. And as populations flee the cities to the suburbs, the city must grab more and more power. Even on the local level, we see centralized power-grabbing, anti-republican principles at work.

The popular opinion holds, says Kotler, that our cities have been growing. But this is incorrect; they are not growing, but annexing other communites. He cites the example of Philadelphia, which was two square miles in 1854. Then the state legislature obliterated neighboring political entities. Philadelphia increased in area to 129.714 square miles, where it has remained ever since. "We can hardly speak of Philadelphia as growing in size," claims Kotler, "when it expanded only once. This is not growth in our normal sense of the word, but a territorial seizure."[3]

Oddly enough, it was the promise of economic opportunities that brought about the acquiescence of the people to join the cities in the first place; but neighborhoods such as Harlem, New York, fell into decay instead.

The solution, according to Kotler, is to return the power to the neighborhoods. Seen on a national scale from the federal government down to the local level, this is the first big step to reverse the flow of power from the central government to the states, then to the people themselves. This is how to return to first principles, to republican government. The capacity for self-government, after years of being ruled, must be developed all over again.

Of course it will not be easy. There is nothing more terrifying to bureaucrats than the prospect of losing control over the lives of their clients. To lose these small opportunities for tyranny means the loss of the personal power they have nourished for years, warns Kotler.

The purpose of neighborhood action today should be to wrest control of local affairs, for local deliberation, from the state and federal governments—to regain self-rule. The struggle will require a determined and effectively organized neighborhood, well-grounded in first principles.

In sum, the sizes of the federal and state governments are too large to be effective protectors of our lives, liberties, and property. De Tocqueville realized the problem over 140 years ago, when he said that a great republic will always be exposed to more perils than a small one, and "the history of the world affords no instance of a great nation retaining the form of republican government for a long series of years."[4] Therefore, it is imperative that our governments be reduced in size, as power is returned to the hands of the citizens.

Here is a final warning on living under any form of government other than a republic. It appeared during the debates on ratification of the Constitution, in the *Philadelphia Independent Gazetteer* on October 5 and November 30, 1787 and was signed "Centinel": "All the blessings of liberty and the dearest privileges of freemen are now at stake and dependent on your present conduct.... If the united states are to be melted down into one empire, it becomes you to consider whether such a government, however constructed, would be practicable, consistent with freedom? It is the opinion of the greatest writers that a very extensive country cannot be governed on democratical principles, on any other plan than a confederation of a number of small republics, possessing all the powers of internal government, but united in the management of their foreign and general concerns. It would not be difficult to prove, that anything short of despotism could not bind so great a country under one government; and that whatever plan you might, at first setting out, establish, it would issue in despotism."[5]

NOTES ON REPUBLIC, CHAPTER IX

1. Op. Cit., P. 321.
2. *Democracy in America*, Vol. I, Author's Preface, P. cxii.
3. (New York: The Bobbs-Merrill Co., Inc.,) 1969, Pp. 15-16, 18-20.
4. *Democracy in America*, Vol. I, Pp. 160-61.
5. *Annals of America*, Vol. 3,Pp. 150, 152-3.

X

Democracy

I cling with a firmer hold to the belief that for democratic nations to be virtuous and prosperous, they require but to will it.
ALEXIS DE TOCQUEVILLE

This chapter is about popular government, democracy, majority rule, and equality, which are all related. It will round out the discussion on what is a democratic Republic. But more importantly, it warns about the perils of unlimited democracy.

It seems that all governments have been perverted at one time or another. Royalty became tyranny; aristocracy turned into oligarchy; constitutional government declined into democracy. None of them had the common good in mind. But in a democracy, on which we will concentrate, everyone has the vote, so justice becomes the application of numerical not proportionate equality. For instance, "...the poor have more power than the rich, because there are more of them, and the will of the majority is supreme."[1] This is the major problem of a democracy.

Seneca warned that a democracy is more cruel than wars and tyrants because, without checks and balances, it becomes mob rule, chaos, and dictatorship. This he claims is the result of bold and unscrupulous leaders being choosen by the popular vote, who have curried favor with the people by giving them other men's property.

Herein lies this inherent problem in all purely democratic states. If the will of the majority is supreme, they can vote away the rights of the minority, of the individual, in addition to their own rights as well, whether they realize it or not. Thus the spirit of extreme equality leads to despotic power and corruption as witnessed in Soviet Russia today or during the French Revolution, where equality at any cost was the goal.

In addition, since it requires every citizen to be able to say "no" at the power it holds in the vote, to respect the rights of everyone and not demand more for themselves, there is no government so subject to civil wars and internal agitations as democratic or popular government.

The Founding Fathers were well aware of this problem. *The Federalist* No. 51 stated "If a majority be united by a common interest the rights of the minority will be insecure." This led Madison to conclude that democracies have ever been spectacles of turbulence and contention; have been ever found incompatible with personal security or the rights of property; and have in general been as short in their lives as they have been violent in their deaths. Therefore, Hamilton proudly proclaimed the United States had a republican form of government because "real liberty is never found in a despotism or in the extremes of Democracy." And lastly, Sam Adams reminded his countrymen: "Remember, democracy never lasts long. It soon wastes, exhausts and murders itself. There never was a democracy that did not commit suicide." The purpose of the Bill of Rights was actually to hobble the majority as well as restrain the federal government.

In democracies, this reign of tyranny of the majority is far worse than any other type of tyranny because when society is itself the tyrant, it leaves few means of escape. It has a way of imposing its own ideas and practices as rules of conduct on those who dissent from the majority. It prevents the development and formation of any individuality not in harmony with its ideas. It thus becomes a more formidable type of political despotism. In short, one of the greatest dangers of democracy lies in class legislation.

In fact, the whole drift of our laws is tending toward the absolute prohibition of all ideas that diverge in the slightest from society's preconceived opinions. The national philosophy is erecting conformity into one of the noblest of virtues while relegating the free functioning of an individual personality into a capital crime against society. This can be seen in the public school system, where from the earliest grades, social conformity is heavily stressed over individual ability. It is more important to get along with others, than to be right or different.

Hayek asserts that when right is what the majority says it is, democracy degenerates into demagoguery. Therefore, "if it is to survive, democracy must recognize that it is not the fountainhead of justice, and that it needs to acknowledge a conception of justice which does not necessarily manifest itself in the popular view on every particular issue."[2]

De Tocqueville made a study of democracies. He witnessed the French Revolution of the early 1800s, then came to the United States in 1830-31 to study our political system. In 1835 he began publishing his two volumes entitled: *Democracy in America.* They became a success overnight; he was acclaimed the expert on democracies. In the second volume he wrote that a natural tendency of democratic nations, which is extremely dangerous, is that which leads them to despise and undervalue the rights of private persons. Consequently, these rights are often sacrificed without regret and almost always violated without remorse.[3] Victimless crimes are excellent examples of such violations of private rights.

Since it is easier to establish an absolute and despotic government among a people where the conditions of society are equal, despotism appears more likely to occur and to be dreaded in democratic times, concludes de Tocqueville.[4]

One of the consequences of a democracy is that with universal suffrage comes fewer able men. The least enlightened are able to rise to positions of power because they can pander to the will of the majority. Incompetence and mediocrity reign supreme. Indeed, Supreme Court Justice MacLean in 1831, told de Tocqueville "I do not think that with our democracy we could govern the whole Union for long [as a free country], if it formed but one single people."[5]

Part of the problem lies in the fundamental assumption that the powers of the majority have no bounds. This divine right of majorities is a throwback to the days of the divine rights of legislatures, parliaments, and kings. As with all superstitions, this belief in government omnipotence will die hard. Nevertheless, for the majority to coerce the minority into undertaking any acts against its will, is nothing less than gross tyranny.

John C. Calhoun cautioned us that "no government based on the naked principle that the majority ought to govern,... can preserve its liberty even for a single generation... Let it never be forgotten that, where the majority rules without restriction, the minority is the subject." (This pertains to the majority of government employees over private employees, religious followers over non-religious, non-gun owners over gun owners, non-drug users over drug users, etc.) " it follows necessarily that where the numerical majority has the sole control of the government, there can be no constitution, as constitution implies limitation or restriction."[6] Control of the government should be interpreted as control of special interest groups.

Four hundred years ago a professor in England by the name of Alexander Fraser Tyler examined the bitter fruits of democracy. He concluded that a democracy cannot exist as a permanent form of government. It can exist only until the voters discover that they can vote themselves largess out of the public treasury. From that moment on the majority always votes for the candidate promising the most benefits from the public treasury—with the result that democracy always collapses over a loose fiscal policy, always to be followed by dictatorship. This seems to be where the United States is headed, as all forms of justice and prudence are being discarded as fast as they can be "sold."

Our Founding Fathers had a deep fear of democracies. In fact, the Constitution was a result of a powerful reaction *against* democracy. Hamilton made it clear that "if government is in the hands of the few, they will tyrannize over the many; if in the hands of the many, they will tyrannize over the few. It ought to be in the hands of both, and they be separated. This separation must be permanent.'' Otherwise, democracy inevitably lapses into tyranny.

Under a democracy a new race of men springs up to govern the nation. They are the hunters after popularity—men ambitious, not of the honor so much as of the profits of office; the demagogues with non-existing principles who follow, not what is right, but what leads to a temporary vulgar applause. There is a very great danger that these men have curried so much popular favor that they already rule the nation.

No discussion of democracy, however, would be complete without examining the term ''equality.'' The only kind of equality conducive to liberty is equality before the law. But what was once considered equality, where men were free to work and prosper, has been perverted to mean equality where men are assured an equal start and guaranteed some reward.

Equality has also been suggested to mean that all have a right to vote, which leads to majority rule. But only responsible, tax-paying citizens should have the right to vote. He who pays for government ought to be the one with a vote on how his money is to be spent. The slogan of the Federalist Party was ''Those Who Own the Country Ought to Govern It.'' In fact, if the law were restricted to protecting individual rights and organized justice, the vote would not be so popular. If it only carried responsibility, not plunder, only responsible citizens would want the obligation to vote and they could and would guard their rights very jealously.

As Voltaire once said, ''Equality is at once the most natural and most chimerical thing in the world: natural when it is limited to rights, unnatural when it attempts to level goods and powers.'' Hence, equality seems to be merely idealized envy. This is where the passion for equality ends by destroying itself.

That is it in a nutshell. Equality is simply the envy by the poor of the rich. But, ''you can't make the poor richer by making the rich poorer,'' as Churchill said.

To listen to those who would make equality a condition essential to liberty is to destroy both liberty and equality before the law, because to try to equalize the qualities and attributes of men, which are not subject to measurement at all, must logically lapse, again, into despotism.

Rand points out that this conception of equality gives rise to a perversion of political rights into ''economic'' rights. These new economic rights entail a right to a job, to make a living, to a decent home, to adequate medical care, to a good education, and to protection from the fears of old age, sickness, accidents, and unemployment, as taken from the 1960 Democratic Party platform and formerly called President Roosevelt's economic bill of rights.

Just as bad money drives out good money (Gresham's Law), so bad laws drive out good laws. To proclaim and advocate economic rights is to negate and destroy the concept of political rights.

The question to ask of these new "economic rights" is: At whose expense? If one part of the nation can lay claim on the property and production of another part, then clearly all semblance of freedom and individual rights have vanished, as there can be no such thing as "the right to enslave." Indeed, the issue is political rights *versus* economic rights; political rights or no rights. It is either/or. One destroys the other. Therefore, while the people are clamoring about "economic rights," the concept of political rights is vanishing.[7]

As the reader can see by now, a democracy is but a mob and equality is merely a disguise of the envious to legally plunder the wealth of others. This is the point at which today's equality-seekers, socialists, egalitarians, etc. have brought the country in the name of equality and democracy.

In *Business Week* magazine a series of three articles was written during the month of December, 1975, by John Cobbs. They clearly state the purpose and goals of modern equality seekers, known as egalitarians. "They want the government," writes Cobbs, "to use its powers to restructure the economic system and equalize its rewards, giving to the poor as a matter of *right.* (P. 62)

These new rights are to include a redistribution of "wealth and incomes, to equalize differences in education and family backgrounds, and to override the classic principle that what a man consumes must be determined by what he produces or what he owns. To achieve uniformity and equality, they are prepared to sacrifice diversity and individual liberty. The egalitarian movement is essentially authoritarian," reports Cobbs.

Please let that sink in for a moment. Yes, you read it right. *They* are willing to sacrifice your abilities, wealth and individual rights to attain their goals: your production and/or wealth--your enslavement!

If inequality and liberty go together, then equality and slavery go together. The United States achieved political equality in its Constitution, which protected the freedom, the rewards, and the incentives for every individual's achievement, each to the extent of his ability and ambition, thus raising the intellectual, moral and economic state of the whole society.[8] But this modern type of equality is nothing less than communism, where liberty is exchanged for security and slavery. This is the final end of a democracy, where the ultimate quest for equality ends where the majority rules and rights are anything anyone or any group says they are. This is the vilest form of tyranny and despotism because there can be no escape, nowhere to turn for justice. Despotism today parades as the honorable will of the majority. The egalitarian movement is the ultimate movement for universal *in*justice. At this point it might be fitting for the reader to re-read the chapter on revolution; this is how one is produced.

Before concluding, another issue relevant here should be brought up. That is, in a free economic system the wealthy are merely somewhat ahead of the rest in the material advantages which they enjoy. It is crucial to realize that it is the wealthy who support new ideas in the marketplace. Without their support most modern labor-saving devices, such as dishwashers, frost-free refrigerators, and microwave ovens, to name but a few, would never have become available as commonplace household items.

In sum, Jose Ortega y Gasset, author of *The Revolt of the Masses,* observed: "What before would have been considered one of fortune's gifts, inspiring humble gratitude towards destiny, was converted into a right, not to be grateful for, but to be insisted on." The conclusion y Gasset draws is: "The mob goes in search of bread, and the means it employs is generally to wreck the bakeries."

NOTES ON DEMOCRACY, CHAPTER X

1. Op. Cit., P. 520.
2. *Constitution of Liberty*, P. 117.
3. Op. Cit.,P. 326.
4. IBID., P. 322.
5. *Journey to America*, P. 93.
6. Op. Cit., Pp. 198-201.
7. *Capitalism: The Unknown Ideal*, P. 294.
8. Ayn Rand, *The Objectivist*, "The Age of Envy," Part I, July, 1971, P. 13.

XI

Politicians

Men by their constitutions are naturally divided into two parties: 1. Those who fear and distrust the people, and wish to draw all powers from them into the hands of the higher classes. 2. Those who identify themselves with the people, have confidence in them, cherish and consider them as the most honest and safe, although not the most wise depository of the public interests. In every country these two parties exist; and in every one where they are free to think, speak and write, they will declare themselves.
THOMAS JEFFERSON

No political discussion on justice would be complete without including politicians. Specifically, this chapter addresses itself to good and bad politicians, their "art" of compromising, and a call to battle.

To begin, men who are honest and simple are difficult to deceive because their simplicity thwarts the use of lures and ingenious pretexts to deceive them. Hence, peace, unity and equality are the enemies of political subtleties and intrigues.

Since "implicit faith belongs to fools," as Sidney counsels, truth is comprehended by examining principles. Likewise, good and wise magistrates do not grow up like mushrooms; great judgment is required in choosing them. And as all principles are knowable, it is our own fault if we do not come to a certain knowledge of them. Honest, simple and wise men are a product of a thinking, reasoning society. They are a reflection of the people who elect them, where "the best men make themselves," says Patrick Henry.

Henry prophecied of his fellow countrymen, "If they are wise, they will be great and happy. If they are of a contrary character, they will be miserable. Righteousness alone can exalt them as a nation. Reader! whoever thou art, remember this; and in thy sphere practise virtue thyself, and encourage it in others."

In the same context, Henry along with Jefferson and Washington, believed that a public office was neither to be sought nor refused. They believed that one might not refuse to obey the orders of his countrymen. Election to office was regarded as a call to duty, rather than a political reward."In a virtuous government," said Jefferson, "public offices are...burdens to those appointed to them...." Men were re-elected only if their previous labors had been satisfactory and acceptable. Renewable terms were not popular. Henry especially was averse to them, because "a man who is fond of office, and has his eye upon re-election, will be courting favour and popularity, at the expense of his duty."

A good man for public office was recognized by Sophocles (495-406 B.C.) in "Antigone" as a man who deals in fairness with his own, so he can manifest justice in public affairs.

Bailyn, in his *The Origins of American Politics,* helps us to distinguish true patriots from office-seekers looking for a safe job. The first test is that "patriots never seek office; they have it thrust upon them.... They do not seek office because they do not need office; independent in wealth and opinion, they cannot be bought or meanly influenced. They are...lovers of virtue."[1]

The test of time also distinguishes the good office-holder, who thinks it a great part of his duty, by precept and example, to educate the youth in a love of virtue and truth and to seek union and harmony in the public. The demagogue, on the other hand, who fancies he is not there for the benefit of the people, but the people for his benefit, stirs dissension. He does not inquire what he may do for the people, but how he may profit from them. He declares the active defense of justice to be "sedition and rebellion," and strives to diminish any strength, virtue, power, and courage which he knows to be his enemy. He is fearful of the truth, always endeavoring to establish falsehood and dishonesty, to corrupt youth, and to bring the people to such a plight that they neither care nor dare to vindicate their rights. The bad magistrate will try to multiply his duties in order to increase his power and to buy votes, thereby influencing elections and destroying the liberties of the people. He will of necessity seek to increase taxes. He will use every instrument available to extend the lives of official programs, laws, and regulations.

Therefore, republics must derive their strength and vigor from *popular and critical examination* into the actions of their magistrates.

To Locke and the Founding Fathers there was no alternative to thinking and responsibility. It was expected of free men to be on guard against possible usurpations and tyrannies. Today, however, Americans are to busy to see the threats to their lives and liberties. They are complacent and content to hear familiar catch-phrases. When all their liberties are gone and their very lives threatened, they will not know how, when, or where it happened.

Nock hits us where it hurts, in our intelligence. He quotes the political economist, Michel Chevalier, who observed that the American people have "the morale of an army on the march." "An army on the march," adds Nock, "has no philosophy; it views itself as a creature of the moment."[2]

This is the philosophy of pragmatism—of short-range thinking. It explains why politicians use no long-range thinking to solve problems, and why the country is suffering from incorrect, incoherent government interference.

Furthermore, as long as politicians never explicitly state their aims, they can go further than any dictator, without trouble or question. President Franklin Roosevelt never publicly declared: "The state creates rights." But he acted as though he believed it were true and no one opposed him.

What if Congress should defend the actions of the Internal Revenue Service, The Federal Bureau of Investigation, and the Central Intelligence Agency by publicly announcing Hegel's dictum that "the State alone possess rights, because it is the strongest." One can hardly imagine that the public would swallow that without a great deal of disgust. But has not Congress said that implicitly, by condoning those agencies' "questionable" actions. Nowhere are these national police forces' activities curbed.

Nock observes that "the American is the most unphilosophical of beings. The rationalization of conduct in general is most repugnant to him; he prefers to emotionalize it. He is indifferent to the theory of things, so long as he may rehearse his formulas; and so long as he can listen to the patter of his litanies, no practical inconsistency disturbs him-indeed, he gives no evidence of even recognizing it as inconsistency."[3]

De Tocqueville noticed the same phenomenon upon his visit to the United States: "The spirit of the Americans is averse to general ideas; it does not seek theoretical discoveries."[4]

This habit of noncritical thinking by Americans is reflected in their elected officials. For instance, there is no instance of party adherence to a fixed principle or to a political theory. This could not occur if individuals applied the virtues of honesty and justice, which they expect in their private dealings, to their representatives in government. Here is the crux of the problem. It is one of morality. The public does not expect nor demand high moral standards of its government; thus, it does not receive them. The advice of Will Rogers not to take politicians seriously seems to have been totally accepted. Consequently, we witness today such a display of immorality, dishonesty, deceit, injustice, and overall lack of integrity, that no honest citizen would be caught dead running for public office.

Nowadays the purpose of elections seems to be to make the government a broker in pillage while the election is sort of an advanced auction sale of stolen goods.[5] "The general upshot of all this is," according to Nock, "that we see politicians of all schools and stripes behaving with the obscene depravity of degenerate children; like the loose-footed gangs that infest the railway-yards and purlieus of gas-houses, each group tries to circumvent another with respect to fruit accruing to acts of public mischief."[6]

Could this continue if instead of shaking our heads in dismay when such acts are publicized, we displayed indignation and expected, no, demanded, an explanation? And when none was forthcoming, or an unsatisfactory one was offered, we kicked the scoundrels out of office? No, dear reader, politicians get away with nothing less than murder because we evade the issue. The "righteousness" of which Henry spoke is nonexistent today. The moral depravity reflected in all levels of government is our own.

Such toleration becomes a habit. And as Jefferson warned us, our rulers will become corrupt and the people careless, their rights disregarded, when we forget ourselves in the sole faculty of making money. Even de Tocqueville could not help but notice that the American statesmen of 1830 were very inferior to those who stood at the head of affairs fifty years before.

Andrew Jackson, in his farewell speech in 1837, warned the people, "It is from within, among yourselves...that factions will be formed and liberty endangered."[7] There will always be designing politicians trying to curry favor and purchase influence, but how can they get away with it if we do not sell our vote to them? Moral law is written on the tablets of eternity—justice is justice, honor is honor, truth is truth, and a good magistrate is a good magistrate. The principles of true politics are merely those of morality enlarged.

How low have we actually fallen? Spencer, generations ago, described the legislature as having "lapsed into the hands of wire-pullers; that its doings turned upon the contests of office-seekers; that political action was everywhere vitiated by the intrusion of a foreign element holding the balance between parties; that electors, instead of judging for themselves, were habitually led to the polls in thousands by their 'bosses'; and that respectable men were driven out of public life by the insults and slanders of professional politicians."[8]

How did this vicious turnabout take place? Paterson points out that prior to the Civil War a man seeking political honors usually expected to do so at some financial loss to himself since he lived by his private means. Under this system, men of intelligence, integrity, and good taste–the productive character–would be inclined to enter public life. The productive man is aware that the cost of government is an expense charged upon production through taxation; he does not like to live at the expense of others. The cost of government is always in inverse proportion to the liberty and prosperity of the citizens. Hence, the best men are found in politics only when it is burdensome, unpompous, and at their own expense.

In contrast, today's office-seekers are accustomed to living off unearned incomes; they only know of the parasitical way in politics. Consequently, government has become a place of ostentatious public buildings and large salaries and embassies.

Adam Smith described a politician as "that insidious and crafty animal...whose councils are directed by momentary fluctuations of affairs." Lord Acton concluded that "the danger is not that a particular class is unfit to govern. Every class is unfit to govern."

How has the country gotten itself into such a political dilemma? In a word, "compromise." Some say the "art" of politics is the art of compromising. That is false; the evil of compromising principles cannot be overly stressed. For in any collaboration between two men (or two groups) who hold different basic principles, it is the more evil or irrational one who wins. In any compromise with evil, evil always wins.

For instance, the United Nations is allegedly dedicated to peace, freedom, and human rights. But it includes, among others, Soviet Russia, the bloodiest dictatorship and mass-murderer in all history. Thus, the U.N. has sanctioned the morals of the communist world. The U.N. has served injustice by delivering a larger part of the earth's populace into the power of Russia than Russia could ever have conquered by outright brute force. And the Western world, led by the United States, has, in essence and deed, sanctioned it.

This is a prime example of the "art" of compromising. It could never have happened if men behaved justly; a criminal is not to be treated as a friend. It insults one's true friends and insults oneself.

To quote Rand: "In any compromise between food and poison, it is only death that can win. In any compromise between good and evil, it is only evil that can profit."[9] The true answer to political maneuvering is never to compromise principles; stand up for what is right and "don't give an inch!"

Davy Crockett, who was a Congressman for three terms, learned the difference between right and wrong from a constituent of his. In the 1830s while stumping for support, a farmer refused to vote for Crockett. Upon questioning, the farmer replied that previously Crockett had voted to appropriate $20,000 to help some residents of Washington who had been made homeless by a fire. He told Crockett that he had no right to spend taxpayers money for that reason; it set a dangerous precedent. If the representatives were truly sympathetic and truly honest to the Constitution, they would have raised contributions from their own pockets. Years later, a similar appropriation arose in the House and Crockett rose to the occasion. He said he could not let his respect for the deceased lead him into an act of injustice to the living. He repeated his lesson on fiscal responsibility and said he would contribute a week's salary to the widow if every other member did; that ended the matter. There is a right and wrong to every issue.

What is the solution to today's dilemma? In 1974, the founder and prime mover behind the Committee to Establish the Gold Standard, Howard S. Katz, wrote an article for his newsletter *The Gold Bug.* The article was entitled: "A Question of Values." In essence, it was a call to arms; it could have been entitled: "Now is the Time for All Good Men to Come to the Aid of Their Country." The following passages are from Katz's splendid work:

> Consider the time in human history immediately after the discovery of agriculture. A young man of that time could choose a livelihood in agriculture, or he could choose the traditional livelihood of hunting and gathering. Here clearly the rational choice for an ambitious and competent man was the new agriculture....
>
> Now turn the pages of history forward to the time of the industrial revolution with the inventions of the new machines. At this time the choice was between agriculture and industry.... *Now it was industry which allowed* a great increase in wealth and opportunity....
>
> Every once in a while world conditions undergo a major change which necessitates a change in our system of values. Before the discovery of agriculture a youth could look forward to a life of hunting and gathering, just as his father had done. But after the discovery of agriculture he was faced with a choice; this choice was of a moral nature. It required of him a re-*evaluation*. That is, it required him to *reassess his values* and to do so *by a rational process.* All of the non-rational factors—conservatism, fear of the new, family pressure, the opinion of the community, simple inertia—worked to persuade him of the incorrect choice. It was only a rational decision on the subject of values which gave him the proper choice.
>
> It has been often remarked concerning the great amount of talent in the field of politics in the late 18th century...and the total lack of talent in the 19th century, where we find example after example of dull mediocre presidents and statesmen....
>
> The reason for this was that between the late 18th and 19th centuries *a major change had occurred in world conditions.* The greatest value in the world in the 18th century was freedom.... *The great minds of the 18th*

century turned themselves to the question of freedom, and thus to the sphere of politics; the great minds of the 19th century turned to business.

The youth who in 1840 chose a career in politics was a dolt [just as was the youth who chose hunting rather than agriculture.] But the youth of 1840 who chose a career in business, in particular one of the new fields opening up at the time, showed *a correct understanding and a great deal of vision.*

Now what is important to understand is that our age has seen a fundamental change in world conditions making it essentially different from the world of the 19th century. Most such fundamental changes in human history are advances; however, our age has seen a regression. *This regression is the loss of freedom which has so blighted the 20th century and constitutes the principal problem of our time.*

The reason freedom is so important is that *it is a prerequisite* to any other value.... For men living as serfs under the control of a government bureaucrat there is simply no point to working for any value. Why try to build a business when a government edict can destroy it at any time...

We conclude then that... *the loss of freedom is the crucial fact of our age*, the fundamental change....

It follows then that, *for people who recognize this,* there is a *re-evaluation* required.... We cannot simply follow along pursuing the goals and values taught us by our parents;...they are not the proper goals for our time.

What is required for our time is *pursuit of the value of freedom.* This is the goal which is properly realistic for our age. *To pursue other values* which are based on freedom at a time when freedom itself is slipping away *is futile and impractical.*

There is no protection for those who place themselves in the power of evil. There is no security in subjugation. It is not safe to give up one's freedom.

It is the struggle for freedom which is the real thing in the world today.... *It is the moral which is truly practical.*

There is only one hope left—to stop the tide of tyranny, to fight ideas with ideas, to take a stand for liberty and justice. As the Reverend John Horne said during the American Revolution, "We are stones of one arch, and must stand or fall together."

How can we elect weak, lazy men to office and expect a strong and just government? Now is the time for honest individuals to pursue political careers. All honest men are desperately needed to bring justice and rationality back into government. De Tocqueville recognized the problem nearly 150 years ago when he admitted that it is painful to perceive how much lower we have sunk than our forefathers, since we allow things to pass, under the color of justice and the sanction of law, which violence alone has imposed upon us.[10]

For example, Congress now introduces about *25,000* pieces of legislation annually; only about 1.6 percent are enacted into law (thank goodness). But to accomplish this vast output of legislation, the cost is hundreds of millions of dollars. In addition to the Congressional Record is a book equally as large called the Federal Register. It includes Executive Orders, of which there are almost *12,000* on the books today. What we are witnessing, therefore, is a massive defection of responsibility on the part of Congress in the quest for total legislation, which can end only in total slavery!

Regarding political parties, it would not hurt to relegate them to a thing of the past. Indeed, Jefferson, ever an individualist, never valued political organizations or government power for their own sake; he believed in individuals and local units of manageable size. He was sought after by the people because he was a man of integrity, not party. He said, "I never submitted the whole system of my opinions to the creed to any party of men whatsoever in religion, in philosophy, in politics or in anything else where I was capable of thinking for myself. Such an addiction is the last degradation of a free and moral agent. If I could not go to heaven but with a party, I would not go there at all."

If to achieve happiness and prosperity, an individual ought to possess industry, integrity, justice and prudence, then good government needs no less the same. For government is merely morality enlarged. Government requires and deserves no less effort to achieve success than any other enterprise.

In the new world, said de Tocqueville, a man had no enemy other than himself, and in order to be happy and to be free he had only to determine that he would be so. It still holds true today. Sure it is a struggle; no one says it's easy. But the harder the struggle, the more glorious the victory.

In the same vein, No. 70 of *Cato's Letters* declares, "You are born to Liberty, and it is your Interest and Duty to preserve it." Free men of reason and spirit, awake your spirit, exert your reason, assert your freedom. "You have a right to address your Representatives—to propose your thoughts and Grievances—to be heard and relieved of any suffering."

In conclusion, "If there is anything certain in human affairs, it is that valuable acquisitions are only to be retained by the continuation of the same energies which gained them. Things left to take care of themselves inevitably decay."[11]

NOTES ON POLITICIANS, CHAPTER XI

1. Op. Cit., P. 143.
2. *Our Enemy, the State*, P. 12.
3. Op. Cit., P. 12.
4. *Democracy in America*, Vol. I, P. 315.
5. *Reason*, Box 40105, Santa Barbara, California, September, 1976 P. 24.
6. Op. Cit., P. 77.
7. *Essays on Freedom and Power*, Pp. 206-07.
8. *The Man Versus the State*, P. 66.
9. *Capitalism: The Unknown Ideal*, P. 148.
10. *Democracy in America*, Vol. I, P. 105.
11. Mill, P. 334.

XII

Free Enterprise

Why should we fetter commerce? ... Let her be free as air. She will range the whole creation and return on the four winds of Heaven to bless the land with plenty.
PATRICK HENRY

With this chapter begins the development of the relationship between politics and economics, for they form the foundation of society. Individual rights and free enterprise produce freedom and prosperity. Large compulsive government and socialism produce slavery and poverty. These systems are not interchangeable. Either society respects life, liberty, and property, or it does not. This chapter explains what the free enterprise system is in theory, and why it is of vital importance to the maintenance of a free society and a high standard of living.

The free enterprise system is a relatively new phenomenon, a development of the past few hundred years. Before this development, governments were considered to be in charge of commerce and trade. Free enterprise was officially introduced by Adam Smith's *Wealth of Nations,* published in 1776.

The freeing of commerce from government regulation actually took place before 1776, because it was recognized that the spirit of free trade produces in the mind of a man a certain sense of justice and that commerce is naturally attended to with frugality, economy, moderation, labor, prudence, tranquillity, and order. It was also recognized that if these virtues are banished, as a result of government interference, then avarice possesses the whole community.[1]

Most people agree that trade and commerce are necessary and good. What they cannot decide upon is how much freedom to allow businessmen, and how much government regulation is needed to keep merchants "honest." This chapter will argue the case in favor of absolute "laissez-faire," hands-off free enterprise, as was intended by our Founding Fathers. For there is no mention of regulating domestic trade in the Constitution.

How free was the state of business around the 1800s in the United States? The answer is surprising: At the request of Congress, the Secretary of the Treasury, Albert Gallatin, prepared a report on the progress of manufacturing in the U.S. It was submitted to the House of Representatives on April 19, 1810. Here are some excerpts:

> "The revenue of the United States being principally derived from duties on the importation of foreign merchandise;...the frugality of government have rendered unnecessary any oppressive taxes....
>
> No cause, indeed, has perhaps more promoted in every respect the general prosperity of the United States than the absence of those systems of internal restrictions and monopoly which continue to disfigure the state of society in other countries.... Industry is in every respect *perfectly free* and *unfettered;* every species of trade, commerce, art, profession, and manufacture being *equally open to all, without requiring any* previous regular apprenticeship, admission, or *license*... [Americans] carry on with complete success even those branches for which a monopoly had heretofore been considered essentially necessary.
>
> The same principle has...a decided superiority to the citizens of the United States over the inhabitants of countries *oppressed by taxes, restrictions,* and *monopolies.*[2]

In short, government had no business in the affairs of businessmen. Men relied on each other's honesty, integrity, and reputation. That air of freedom and trust launched the greatest economic achievements in mankind's history. The highest standard of living was achieved in record time by an upstart, new nation, not because of government, but because of lack of government meddling. It was freedom from government interference that was the cause.

The Founding Father set it up that way. They had full confidence in man's ability to produce wealth. They would have been very proud of the accomplishments of their posterity.

Paine fully understood and appreciated free enterprise. When persuading a committee to leave commerce free from its interference, he said, "The committee are not so capable of taking care of commerce, as commerce is capable of taking care of itself. The farmer understands farming, and the merchant understands commerce; and as riches are equally the object of both, there is no occasion that either should fear that the other will seek to be poor. The more money the merchant has, so much the better for the farmer who has produce to sell; and the richer the farmer is, so much the better for the merchant, when he comes to his store."

Paine understood mankind far better than mankind understood (and understands) itself. In the second part of his "Rights of Man," Paine describes the interdependency man has upon man and how it needs no government interference or regulation. In an environment of freedom and trust, mankind can take care of itself superbly well: A "great part of that order which reigns among mankind is not the effect of government. It had its origin in the principles of society and the natural constitution of man. It existed prior to government, and would exist if the formality of government was abolished. The mutual dependence and reciprocal interest which man has upon man, and all parts of a civilized community upon each other, create that great chain of connection which holds it together. The landholder, the farmer, the manufacturer, the merchant, the tradesman, the every occupation, prospers by the aid which each receives from the other, and from the whole. Common interest regulates their concerns, and forms their laws; and the laws which common usage ordains, have a greater influence than laws of government. In fine, society performs for itself almost every thing which is ascribed to government." And we might add, it performs them better, faster, and cheaper.

Paine was not the only Founding Father who understood the magnificence of free enterprise. Jefferson, as a follower of Adam Smith, was quite articulate on the subject: "Instead of embarassing commerce under piles of regulating laws, duties and prohibitions, could it be relieved from all its shackles in all parts of the world, could every country be employed in producing that which nature has best fitted it to produce, and each be free to exchange with others mutual surpluses for mutual wants, the greatest mass possible would then be produced of those things which contribute to human life and human happiness; the numbers of mankind would be increased, and their condition bettered." Private enterprise and economy were "among the first and most important Republican virtues," and "agriculture, manufactures, commerce and navigation, the four pillars of our prosperity, are the most thriving when left most free to individual enterprise."

(This chapter is not an economic treatise on free enterprise. It discusses the political-economic theory behind it. For a more comprehensive study of free enterprise, the reader is referred to the author's prior book, *Why Gold?)*

Basically, free enterprise is an economic system whereby an individual can go into any business he chooses and try to make a success out of it. He is not hampered by license fees, inventory taxes, government regulations, and the like. His sole purpose is to provide a product or a service at a profit.

The key word, of course, is profit. The profit and loss mechanism decides if he will earn money or lose it, including his original capital. This profit and loss system weeds out the failures, those not serving the consumer efficiently. It aids the successful ones by increasing their profits so that they can expand their business. In this way there is a minimum amount of capital lost. The system always favors the efficacious businessman. The consumer benefits from quality merchandise at lower prices from reputable businessmen.

Churchill summed it up: "Private industry runs at a profit and uses the profit to expand producing capacity. Government industry runs at a loss and taxes the substance of the people to pay for its inefficiencies...." Since government's appetite is like that of a glutton (i.e., insatiable), taxes, which come from production and are consequently passed on to consumers in the form of higher prices, continually rise.

Paterson, in her *God of the Machine*, brings up two important facts. One is: "Ideas precede accomplishment," meaning that an idea needs capital behind it to develop and merchandise it. Someone must take a risk in trying something new. The profit incentive of free enterprise supplies the motive. Otherwise, progress would cease.

The second fact which few people realize is that the "United States is the only country on record that has never had a famine since it became a nation."[3] That is quite an accomplishment. It has been made possible by the freedom in which farmers, merchants, and tradesmen each take care of their own business as profitably as possible, which, in turn, supplies the marketplace with goods, services, and food. As Jefferson so aptly remarked, if we waited for directions from Washington, we would all starve.

Where politicians control economic life, totalitarianism exists. Government cannot restore competition, protect consumers, or guarantee low prices. It can only impose restrictions and regulations, doing nothing but harm and wasting precious capital.

Mill realized this, too: "It is but a small portion of the public business of a country which can be well done, or safely attempted, by the central authorities."[4]

Spencer, as an observer of England in the mid-to late 1800s, cogently argues for free enterprise. He witnessed both private enterprise and government authority at work. He concludes, "Private enterprise has done much, and done it well. Private enterprise has cleared, drained, and fertilized the country, and built the towns; has excavated mines, laid out roads, dug canals, and embanked railways; has invented, and brought to perfection ploughs, looms, steam-engines, printing-presses, and machines innumerable; has built our ships, our vast manufactories, our docks; has established banks, insurance societies, and the newspaper press; has covered the sea with lines of steam-vessels, and the land with electric telegraphs. Private enterprise has brought agriculture, manufacturers, and commerce to their present height, and is now developing them with increasing rapidity."[5]

The right interpretation of this phenomenon, says Spencer, is "that among men's desires seeking gratifications, those which have prompted their private activities and their spontaneous co-operations, have done much more towards social development than those which have worked through governmental agencies. That abundant crops now grow where once only wild berries could be gathered, is due to the pursuit of individual satisfactions through many centuries. The progress from wigwams to good houses has resulted from wishes to increase personal welfare; and towns have arisen under the like promptings. Beginning with the traffic at gatherings on occasions of religious festivals, the trading organization, now so extensive and complex, has been produced entirely by men's efforts to achieve their private ends. Perpetually, governments have thwarted and deranged the growth, but have in no way furthered it; save by partially discharging their proper function and maintaining social order.... It is not to the State we owe the multitudinous useful inventions from the spade to the telephone; it was not the State which made possible extended navigation by a developed astronomy; it was not the State which made the discoveries in physics, chemistry, and the rest, which guide modern manufacturers; it was not the State which devised the machinery for producing fabrics of every kind, for transferring men and things from place to place, and for ministering in a thousand ways to our comforts. The world-wide transactions conducted in merchants' offices, the rush of traffic filling our streets, the retail distributing system which brings everything within easy reach and delivers the necessaries of life daily at our doors, are not of governmental origin. All these are results of the spontaneous activities of citizens, separate or grouped. Nay, to these spontaneous activities governments owe the very means of performing their duties. Divest the political machinery of all those aids which Science and Art have yielded it–leave it with those only which State-officials have invented; and its functions would cease."[6]

Spencer sums up his case: "Strong as it looks at the outset, State-agency perpetually disappoints every one. Puny as are its first stages, private effort daily achieves results that astound the world."[7] In sum, prosperity is a result not from law but from the absence of law. The essential truth of the matter is that government interference of any kind, in the economic sphere does immense harm and no good. Justice demands, therefore, that businessmen be left alone.

While in the United States, de Tocqueville observed that "The greatest merit of the government of the United States is that it is *powerless* and *passive.* In the actual state of things, in order to prosper America has no need of skillful direction, profound designs or great efforts. But needs liberty and still more liberty. It is nobody's *interest to abuse it.*"[8]

The United States grew and prospered, nourished by freedom. De Tocqueville saw a "love of prosperity" and a "spirit of enterprise" at work here. Furthermore, since free enterprise is the only economic system that can respect individual rights, it is the only *moral* economic system.

As Jefferson observed, "Were we directed by Washington when to sow and when to reap, we should soon want bread." The Russians are always in want of "bread," and their government always directs the farmer. Success is a result of individuals freely choosing to work together voluntarily, not of governments giving orders and directions, backed by brute force.

The whole point of free enterprise boils down to this: "whoever could make two ears of corn, or two blades of grass, to grow upon a spot of ground where only one grew before, would deserve better of mankind, and do more essential service to his country, than the whole race of politicians put together."[9]

NOTES ON FREE ENTERPRISE, CHAPTER XII

1. Op. Cit., Pp. 21 and 10.
2. *Annals of America*, Vol. 4, Pp. 266-67.
3. Op. Cit., P. 67n.
4. Op. Cit., P. 417.
5. Op. Cit., P. 126.
6. IBID., Pp. 102-03.
7. IBID., P. 147.
8. *Journey to America*, P. 166.
9. Jonathan Swift, *Gulliver's Travels*, P. 78.

XIII

Socialism

[There is a new kind of tyranny. Whereas individual kings' and monarchs' power had limited range, modern bureaucratic governments are all-inclusive. Like a parent they rear their children—but for perpetual childhood, not manhood.] For their happiness such a government willingly labors, but it chooses to be the sole agent and the only arbiter of that happiness; it provides for their security, foresees and supplies their necessities, facilitates their pleasures, manages their principal concerns, directs their industry, regulates the descent of property, and subdivides their inheritance: what remains, but to spare them all the care of thinking and all the trouble of living? [It] gradually robs man of all the uses of himself.

ALEXIS DE TOCQUEVILLE

This chapter on socialism is considerably longer than the prior one on free enterprise because the latter requires only freedom. But socialism is a perverted economic system. It is a system based on the public ownership of the means of production. Its goal is to abolish the institution of private property and to substitute in its place omnipotent government bureaucrats. The government will lead; the people are to follow. Hopefully, this chapter will convince the reader that socialism cannot work under *any* circumstances and leads to affairs far worse than previous ones. It also abolishes individual freedom, prosperity and happiness.

Few people are aware that the founding of America in 1607 was established on true socialist principles–each person contributed the fruit of his labor according to his ability to a common storehouse run by the Virginia company, and from this common store each received produce according to his need.

The results were predictable: "Of the 104 colonists who reached Virginia in May, 1607, only thirty were still alive by that fall, and a similar death rate prevailed among new arrivals for many years. As late as 1616, only 350 colonists remained of a grand total of over 1,600 mmigrants."[1]

In mid-December, 1620, the *Mayflower* landed at Plymouth. Enrced socialist principles produced the same "starving time" hardships—half the colonists were dead by the end of the first winter. Here is a description of the dismal situation by William Bradford, governor of Plymouth in 1621, before reforms were instituted: "this community...was found to breed much confusion and discontent and retard much employment that would have been to their benefit and comfort. For the young men, that were most able and fit for labour and service, did repine that they should spend their time and strength to work for other men's wives and children without any recompense. The strong...had no more in division of victuals and clothes than he that was weak and not able to do a quarter the other could; this was thought injustice," so the work diminished.[2]

In 1623, in order to survive, the colony permitted each family to cultivate a small *private* plot of land for their individual use. "This had very good success," reported Governor Bradford, "for it made all hands very industrious..."

Adam Smith sums up one of the unfair aspects of socialism: "For if all persons in the same kind of work were to receive equal wages, there would be no emulation, and no room left for industry and ingenuity."[3] If the socialist practices of the pilgrims had not given way to private enterprise, there probably would have been no United States of America.

The basic principles of socialism run counter to human nature, rendering it unfit as a social system. Besides, experience should have taught us by now to be on our guard to protect liberty when government's purposes seem most beneficent. Our greatest dangers lurk in the insidious encroachment by men of zeal, but without understanding, *i.e,* advocates of socialism. Current experience confirms that government agents will practice the philosophy of "the end justifies the means" if it will further *their* purposes, no matter whose rights are trampled.

Socialism is a big con game, where government wins and individual liberty loses. It promises cradle-to-grave protection, but who pays for these "benefits"? There is no such thing as a free lunch! Make no mistake about it. Here is the true meaning of socialism, first described by a non-communist Russian scholar: What "distinguishes the Soviet system from all other despotic governments is that...it represents an attempt to found the state on *principles* which are the opposite of those of the rule of law...and it has evolved a *theory* which exempts the rulers from every obligation or limitation."[4]

Second, in the words of a communist theorist: "the fundamental principle of our legislation and our private law, which the bourgeois theorist will never recognize, is: everything is prohibited which is not specially permitted."[5]

Soviet Russia is a socialist nation, as the name states—the Union of Soviet Socialist Republics. It is both communist and socialist; one is the political and the other the economic corollary of the altruist philosophy of self-sacrifice. When Hitler wrote *Mein Kampf* few believed him. When communist and socialist writers tell how they plan to establish a government opposite "the rule of law," they mean to bring back the government of rule of man, or dictatorship. When they say they want to establish a system where "everything is prohibited," they mean to take away all man's rights, except the right to obey—to set up a totally one-sided, authoritative, and unjust social system. When they say these things, believe them. They speak the truth. They are after your lives, liberties, property, and happiness. They are after you. Believe them!

Americans have trouble understanding foreign ideologies because they have been born in freedom. They cannot conceive of being told how to live, where to go, etc. Once, when a visitor from England asked a Texas cowboy, "Where is your master (boss)?" The cowboy replied, "The son-of-a-bitch ain't been born yet!" This is the American sense of life. It differs from all others. This is what socialists are trying to destroy; and they will succeed, too, if Americans do not learn who the enemy is and how he operates.

De Tocqueville realized the difference in Americans nearly 150 years ago: "The American struggles against the obstacles that nature opposes to him; the adversaries of the Russian are men. The former combats the wilderness and savage life; the latter, civilization with all its arms. The conquests of the American are therefore gained by the plowshare; those of the Russian by the sword. The Anglo-American relies upon personal interest to accomplish his ends and gives free scope to the unguided strength and common sense of the people; the Russian centers all the authority of society in a single arm. The principal instrument of the former is freedom; of the latter, servitude."[6] It has not changed.

Spencer reaffirms this interpretation. He says that socialism postulates the doctrine that the citizen has no rights which the State is bound to respect; the only rights he has are those which the State grants him.[7]

This is in direct contradiction to our wonderful Declaration of Independence, which asserts that man has "unalienable" rights, and that governments are instituted "to secure these rights." Here is the crux of the issue. If government gives or repeals rights, they are no longer rights, but privileges. (This is something the backers of the Equal Rights Amendment have yet to learn.) Either man possesses natural, unalienable rights or he is told by his government what his privileges, as a slave, are. He is either free or slave. It is either/or.

There are basically only two types of social systems. One is the rule of status, of forced, government-type cooperation such as a caste system has, namely socialism (communism, fascism, etc.). The other is ruled by contract, of voluntary cooperation, of freedom, namely free enterprise. As opposed to the benefits derived from free enterprise, which we saw in the previous chapter, here are some of the things one would witness living under a socialized society.

One of the basic premises, or promises, of socialism is that there should be no suffering, poverty, unemployment, etc., and that society is to blame for that which exists. Therefore, society, or in reality the government, must take action.

But what happens when government takes over? One would do well to remember the common saying, "What you wish well done you must do yourself," because government agencies tend to increase in size and power, not efficiency. Where private enterprises are taught promptness, by loss of trade, government is habitualy slow to learn. In private enterprise each person tends toward his most competent function. Those unfit or unwilling to compete tend toward government work. Hence, government is made of inferior material. Business serves society cheaply and effectively, whereas government, operating out of another's purse, is extravagant. For example, one has only to think of the post office or other federal buildings; they are usually the newest, finest and costliest around town.

To continue, private enterprise seems always to be flexible to meet emergencies, to adapt to change. Government is unadaptable, regimented and inflexible, never being quite able to change as circumstances require. In private enterprise there is a direct relationship between work performed and wages or profits obtained. In government, this connection is non-existent. There is no direct contact with the consumer. There exists instead an antiseptic environment free from competition. Salaries flow irrespective of work performed and often after work ceases. Bribes, perjury and villainy prevail. With no profit motive, see how government grows. There is always room for more parasites on the public payroll.

The net result is far from the elimination of poverty and suffering. The net result is corruption. Jobs and positions are for sale; the consumer's wishes are ignored. Government becomes obstructive, argumentative, rude, disobedient, and finally contemptable. It is too far removed to be disciplined. A private enterprise, when it becomes unneeded and profitless, dwindles away. Government agencies, even though they have become useless, and often detrimental, continue to thrive.

This bumbling, destructive, obnoxious bureaucracy is what Will Rogers referred to as government, and advised us not to take it seriously. Well, brother, you better. (If not you, then who?) If it is not stopped it grows into despotism, where the tyranny of bureaucracies and the brutality of their members are exhibited in contempt for the citizens. The servants have turned into masters that cannot be discharged, fired or removed. Government so fulfills its judicial function as to ruin many, delude others, and frighten away those who most need succor. In short, justice has been driven away.

Government's responsibility of guarding its citizens against aggresion, either individually or nationally, is a rather straightforward proposition. But "to regulate, directly or indirectly," says Spencer, "the personal actions of those subjects is an infinitely complicated matter." And if it cannot accomplish the first effectively, by what chance can it conceivably accomplish the second?

On the other hand, if the first is to protect the individual from others, then the second must be to protect the individual from himself-against his own stupidity, idleness, rashness, faults, or even immorality. It is not possible for government to protect an individual from the consequences of his own nature and actions. And no honest thinking man would entertain such thoughts.

And while the government is busy meddling in everyone's personal lives, it leaves undone those things which it ought to do. Nowhere is justice served. Instead, its corruptions, follies and terrors of law hamper businessmen and trade, inflict harm on the innocent, let the criminal go free to repeat his crimes, and jail the "social" criminal, and on and on the list goes until the entire social structure is undermined.

Free men should ask: Is current legislation aiming at increasing or decreasing individual freedom? Is government respecting or violating individual rights? One answer is to look at the consequences of the Sixteenth (or Income Tax) Amendment. "Under that Amendment it is competent for Congress not only to confiscate the citizen's last penny, but also to levy punitive taxation, discriminatory taxation, taxation for 'the equalization of wealth' or for any other purpose it sees fit to promote."[8] This is slavery, not freedom; this *is* socialism.

Paterson delves deeper into socialism's inherent wickedness. She begins by saying that although there is no such thing as the "collective man," man has natural and social relations. It is these natural affections and relations socialism denounces. Socialism "suggests shifting personal obligations on to 'Society.' It promotes easy divorce, state support of children, the pleasures of promiscuity; it ends in slavery and violation of personality."[9] Furthermore, the socialist, to attain his objective of power over other men rather than mastery of nature, must stop men thinking, valuing, and judging.

It is this power-lust of politicians that blinds them to the evil mischief they do. Some socialists are honest enough to admit they are after power; most are not. Today, socialists would not dare to try to enslave and tyrannize the United States by outright confiscation of its moral and material values. But they have no fear of doing it by a process of internal corruption.

Rand expresses it this way, "Just as in the material realm the plundering of a country's wealth is accomplished by inflating the currency -so today one may witness the process of inflation being applied to the realm of rights. The process entails such a growth of newly promulgated 'rights' that people do not notice the fact that the meaning of the concept is being reversed. Just as bad money drives out good money, so these 'printing-press rights' negate authentic rights."[10] (Refer to Chapter 4)

Nock calls attention to a most crucial perversion in government, namely, that the state never shows "any disposition to suppress crime, but only to safeguard its own monopoly of crime; one sees no way to differentiate the activities of its founders, administrators, and beneficiaries from those of a professional-criminal class."[11] Consequently, the state always moves slowly and grudgingly toward fullfilling any purpose that accrues to society's advantage (sound currency, simple and few laws, etc.), but moves rapidly toward fulfilling those that accrue to its own advantage (inflation, complex legal and tax systems, etc.).

Nock's conclusion is shocking. While the business of government ought to be to maintain freedom and security, and to make recourse to justice costless, easy and informal, government "on the contrary, is primarily concerned with injustice... hence, as we see daily, its disposition is to put justice as far as possible out of reach, and to make the effort after justice as costly and difficult as it can."[12]

This view of government explains a lot of what we witness happening to our justice system today, a system which is neither swift nor just. It also explains the promulgation of new laws which tend to serve the ends of government (victimless crimes, taxation, etc.) rather than society. Man cannot long remain free under a barrage of unjust laws. Yet there can be no appeal to a socialized government thoroughly entrenched behind its camouflage of laws.

Hayek says we have been "warned by some of the greatest political thinkers of the nineteenth century, by de Tocqueville and Lord Acton, that socialism means slavery... [but] we have so completely forgotten the warning that it scarcely occurs to us that the two things may be connected."[13] Socialists get around this by construing the word freedom as meaning free from want and necessities rather than free from political coercion. This promise of greater freedom is one of their most effective weapons.

Hayek quotes Max Eastman, Lenin's old friend, who admitted that Stalinism *is* socialism.... [it] is worse than fascism, more ruthless, barbarous, unjust, immoral, anti-democratic, unredeemed by any hope or scruple...."[14] Although socialists here recoil when they realize that the true aim of socialism is the destruction of freedom, many will not believe it until the connection has been laid bare in all its horrendous aspects.

Another argument socialists use is that socialism or "central planning" is inevitable. Hayek maintains that organized capital and organized labor are behind this propaganda. Both collaborated on legislation to obtain monopoly profits in government-sponsored and government-protected industries. Religion, too, was "bought off" by the government when it was exempted from income taxes (no separation of church and state).

Furthermore, men can enslave themselves by seeking unwise protection from government. For example businessmen, seeking protective tariffs and subsidies, surrender their freedom of autonomy. Racial groups seeking special economic advantages by law can then be discriminated against by law. Any individual (or group) that seeks special privileges from government does so at the expense of every other citizen.

For some reason people feel they are acting responsibly by delegating their responsibility to groups; to act on behalf of a group seems to free people of moral obligations they would ordinarily feel as individuals. But justice cannot be waived so easily.

Thus we see that socialism, whose main promise is the relief from responsibility, cannot be but amoral in its effects. Our values and virtues must be impaired if we condone shirking our individual responsibility to do "right." If we think that government will set everything right, we have surely become tolerant toward particular abuses and indifferent to individual inequities.

The solution is to begin by attacking the *idea* which is false, the *system* which is unjust; an injustice so insidious and independent of personal contact and intention that each of us profits from it without wishing to do so, and suffers from it without knowing the cause of the suffering.

Socialists base their philosophy on three premises: the inertness of mankind, the omnipotence of the law, and the infallibility of the legislator. Thus they sound like misguided, well-intentioned individuals, but they are, in fact, perverting the law for the benefit of the few.

In the Chapter on Law we established the fact that law ought to be organized justice. What socialists do is to turn the law around to legalize theft. It converts plunder into a right. Instead of checking injustice, law becomes an invincible weapon of injustice. This is done for the benefit of the few persons who make the law, and in proportion to the power they hold.[15]

In case the reader has not connected today's oppressive web of taxation rates and other regulations to the above situation, please do so. Legislators are removing the wealth of one group of citizens and transferring it to another. They take a small fee for this "service," of course. Their published salaries are $42,500 annually, plus expenses. The general expenses for Congress for 1976 jumped over the $1 *billion* mark! Who ever said politics is not a lucrative business? And how about "unconscienable" profits?

Here is how legalized plunder goes undetected. First, politicians count on people's complacency to rely on law to maintain justice, as most people see law and justice as one and the same thing. Thus, in order to make plunder appear just, it is only necessary for law to decree and sanction it.

Second, this confusion of law and justice erases from the unwatchful and unwary mind the distinction between justice and injustice.

Third, the citizen is thus placed in the almost impossible position of choosing between his moral sense or losing his respect for the law. If he holds true to himself, then disrespect for law ensues. When law and morality contradict each other, rebellion or revolution must eventually settle the conflict. Few will wish to see this when judging the law. However, unjust laws legalizing plunder do undermine society.

Finally, instead of rooting out these injustices, legislators make them general, then acceptable, by habitual use. A tragic effect of this perversion of law is that it gives an exaggerated importance to politicians and politics in general, until the people realize that they are being victimized by their own representatives. Until, then, however, the game is safe. (After that, it is "out" with the guillotine.)

By using and hiding behind the law, socialists are spared the shame, scruple, and discovery which their acts would otherwise involve. Thieves and pirates never had it so good.

To learn how to identify what legal plunder is, see if the law takes from some persons what belongs to them, and gives it to other persons to whom it does not belong. See of the law benefits one citizen at the expense of another by doing what the *citizen himself cannot do without committing a crime.*

Then abolish this law without delay, for it is not only an evil itself, but also a source for further evils because it invites reprisals. If such a law is not abolished immediately, it will spread and multiply, eventually developing into a system.

Some of the infinite number of ways legal plunder can be committed are defined by Bastiat: tariffs, legal tender laws, conscription, protection, benefits, grants, subsidies, loans, progressive taxation, public schools, guaranteed jobs, guaranteed profits, minimum wages, victimless crimes, a right to relief, health insurance, retirement income, and so on. "All these plans as a whole—with their common aim of legal plunder—constitute socialism."[16]

Socialism is legal plunder. Socialists desire to practice legal plunder, not illegal plunder. They, like all monopolists, desire to use the law for their own profit.

Socialists ask why the law should not organize labor, education, morals and the like, since it organizes justice. The answer is simply that law and order impose nothing but a negation of action to keep a person within the bounds of justice; he is prohibited from harming others. None of his rights are violated. But when law is active, not passive, it *forces* its will over the individual's. It imposes an alien regulation on labor, education, morals, and so on. Intelligence and responsibility are replaced by law.

"Try to imagine," suggests Bastiat, "a regulation of labor imposed by force that is not a violation of liberty; a transfer of wealth imposed by force that is not a violation of property. If you cannot reconcile these contradictions, then you must conclude that the law cannot organize labor and industry without organizing injustice."[17]

Legal plunder is more visible and more "honest" in communist countries because it is complete plunder, versus socialism, which at first is insidiously disguised and strikes at only a few members of society. Socialism is the "indirect approach to despotism." Whereas reformers, writers on public affairs, and legislators would not attempt to impose direct despotism upon us, they have no qualms about turning to the law to impose their despotism, absolutism, and omnipotence. They desire only to make the laws.[18]

Wallace Johnson, in *A Fresh Look at Patriotism*, observes that present-day socialists in the United States quickly disclaim any intention toward extensive nationalization. Yet their pursuit of government control is relentless. This shift in strategy from direct government ownership to government regulation and control is a political flanking movement of rare effectiveness. A frontal attack on private liberty and property would be stoutly resisted. But a gradual, oblique encroachment on others' individual rights by a series of flanking movements, all in the name of public welfare, are achieving their goal. No Paul Revere will ride. It will all be so plausible and gradual, but in the end, a collectivized, socialized society will be effected.[19]

A man is not free in choice or in action by possession of his rights alone. He must have the liberty to *exercise* those rights, or he is not free. Mere words on a piece of paper are not rights; it is the spirit behind those words, the right to use and exercise them, that amounts to freedom.

De Tocqueville says man allows this to happen because he sees not an individual but the people at large who hold the end of his chain. Here is how de Tocqueville describes a socialist society; see if you would want to live in it:

"After having thus successively taken each member of the community in its powerful grasp and fashioned him at will, the supreme power then extends its arm over the whole community. It covers the surface of society with a network of a small complicated rules, minute and uniform, through which the most original minds and the most energetic character cannot penetrate, to rise above the crowd. The will of man is not shattered, but softened, bent, and guided; men are seldom forced by it to act, but they are constantly restrained from acting. Such a power does not destroy, but it prevents existence; it does not tyrannize [?], but it compresses, enervates, extinguishes and stupefies a people, till each nation is reduced to nothing better than a flock of timid and industrious animals, of which the government is the shepherd.''[20]

NOTES ON SOCIALISM, CHAPTER XIII

1. *Conceived in Liberty,* Vol. I., P. 58.
2. IBID., P. 162.
3. Op. Cit., P. 61.
4. *Constitution of Liberty*, P. 240.
5. IBID.
6. *Democracy in America,* Vol. I., P. 434.
7. Op. Cit., P. x.
8. IBID., P. xii.
9. Op. Cit., P. 95.
10. *Capitalism: The Unknown Ideal*, P. 290.
11. *Our Enemy, The State,* P. 22.
12. IBID., P. 84
13. *The Road to Serfdom,* P. 13.
14. IBID., P. 27.
15. *The Law*, P. 11.
16. IBID., P. 22.
17. IBID., P. 29.
18. IBID., P. 55.
19. (Old Greenwich, Conn.: The Devin-Adair Co., 1976), Pp. 7-8.
20. *Democracy in America*, Vol. II., P. 319.

XIV
Regulations

[If government] descended to the details of application, to the circle of individual interest, freedom would soon be banished from the New World.
ALEXIS DE TOCQUEVILLE

The Ohio Division of Wildlife recently used as many as five agents, including two undercover men, to investigate and prosecute an 11-year-old boy for selling fishing worms and crayfish in his parents' front yard. In two weeks his stand sold $4.50 worth of bait, including that sold to the undercover agents. State regulations in Ohio require a permit to sell bait.
LIBERTARIAN PARTY NEWS, NOVEMBER-DECEMBER, 1976

This chapter begins the final section of the book. These six chapters apply the principles and examples that have been covered throughout the book thus far. These six chapters represent concrete examples of some of the problems that are facing the nation, and their solutions. They are but a small sample. However, they illustrate the paramount evils threatening our lives and liberties. If these evils were stopped–regulation of business, currency depreciation, progressive taxation, public education, and gun control–the majority of injustices and tyrannies, that are plaguing the country and unsuspecting Americans, would cease.

An early example of the benefits of freedom from government regulations and taxes is one that took place in Pennsylvania around 1690. Pennsylvania did not impose all the regulations the other colonies had imposed on business. The fact that an enormously greater freedom had prevailed so much longer in Pennsylvania than in the other colonies gave it a tremendous push toward growth and prosperity.

With a population of only 5,000 in 1700, Philadelphia began a remarkable rise that was to make it one of America's foremost cities. It became the commercial port for the farmers not only of Pennsylvania, but of West New Jersey as well. Farmers and merchants were prospering to such an extent that in 1690 Governor Fletcher of New York had to admit that "the town of Philadelphia in fourteen years' time has become nearly equal to the city of New York in trade and riches"—an unwitting tribute to the propulsive powers of individual freedom, unencumbered by taxes and restrictions, as compared to the crippling effects of monopoly and high taxation in the older colony of New York.[1]

Regulations hurt everybody. Although they are mostly aimed at businessmen, some businessmen profit by government regulations. In fact, they work with government to secure the best of both worlds. This chapter intends to show how regulations tend to corrupt businessmen, interfere with good business practices, waste consumers' money, and enlarge government parasitism.

First, there is always that small percentage of businessmen who find making a profit the most important goal, no matter how they do it. It was either Stalin or Lenin who said a capitalist would sell you the rope by which to hang himself it he thought there was a profit in it.

During the Boston boycott of British goods there was to be found a group of defecting merchants. The Reverend Charles Chauncy of Boston angrily denounced them: "So many of them are so mercenary as to find within themselves a readiness to become slaves themselves, as well as to be accessory to the slavery of others, if they imagine they may by this means serve their own private separate interest."[2]

The history of the railroads in America offers a classical illustration of the evils of government regulations and power. The following discourse is from an article entitled "Notes on the History of American Free Enterprise," in which author Rand writes about the founding of the American railroads. She observed:

> The degree of government help received by any one railroad, stood in direct proportion to that railroad's troubles and failures. The railroads with the worst histories of scandal, double-dealing, and bankruptcy were the ones that had received the greatest amount of help from the government. The railroads that did best and never went through bankruptcy were the ones that had neither received nor asked for government help.....
>
> There were many forms of government help for these projects, such as federal land grants, subsidies, state bonds, municipal bonds, etc. A great many speculators started railroad projects as a quick means to get some government cash, with no concern for the future or the commercial possibilities of their railroads.... Some of those men collected the cash and vanished, never starting any railroad at all...."

The "Big Four" of California on federal subsidies, the Central Pacific (now called Southern Pacific) held a monopoly throughout the state for almost thirty years. It charged exorbitant rates. What made this possible was the power of the California legislature. All competition was forbidden by act of legislation. None of this would have been possible in a free, unregulated economy.

"At the other side of the scale," writes Rand, "the railroad that had the cleanest history, was most efficiently built in the most difficult circumstances, and was responsible, single-handed, for the development of the entire American Northwest, was the Great Northern, built by J.J. Hill without any federal help whatever. Yet Hill was persecuted by the government all his life–under the Sherman Act, for being a monopolist(!)"

Rand quotes from Stewart H. Halbrook's *The Story of American Railroads*, for details on how legal blackmail is handled: "Almost from the first, too, the railroads had to undergo the harassments of politicians and their catchpoles, or to pay blackmail in one way or another. The method was almost sure-fire; the politico, usually a member of a state legislature, thought up some law or regulation that would be costly or awkward to the railroads in his state. He then put this into the form of a bill, talked loudly about it, about how it must pass if the sovereign people were to be protected against the monster railroad, and then waited for some hireling of the railroad to dissuade him by a method as old as man. There is record of as many as thirty-five bills that would harass railroads being introduced at one sitting of one legislature."[3]

It is crucial to realize that when the railroad industry proved it held a promise of tremendous wealth, the legislators began their blackmail schemes, forcing railroad owners to turn to bribery to save their businesses. Railroad owners did not start out by corrupting government. They turned to the practice of bribing legislators in the end only in self-protection.

Rand sums it up by explaining, "It is not a matter of accidental personalities, of 'dishonest businessmen' or 'dishonest legislators.' The dishonesty is inherent in and created by the system. So long as a government holds the power of economic control, it will necessarily create a special 'elite,' an 'aristocracy of pull.' It will attract the corrupt type of politician to the legislature, will work to the advantage of the dishonest businessman, and will penalize and, eventually, destroy the honest and the able."

"The villain in the picture was not the businessman, but the legislator, not free enterprise, but government controls."[4]

The moral to the story is that the sole remedy for the abuse of political power is to limit the power; but when politics corrupt businessmen, legislators invariably demand the enlargement of the political power and more government regulations to stop the corruption government itself created.

To "regulate" businesses diverts attention from the real cause, which is government, to the effects, which are monopoly, higher prices, and/or shoddy goods.

There has and always will be collusion between government and some part of business. The cure is simply to remove the favor-making power from Congress–to separate state and economics and establish laissez-faire (hands-off) free enterprise. Otherwise, politics will continue to corrupt the weaker element of business.

What it does not corrupt, it harms. This is the other side. For the honest businessman trying to run his business competitively, government regulations get in the way, hamper trade, and cost consumers money. "Totalitarian government," says Paterson, "is nothing but political control over economic life." And all excuses for regulations–restore competition, protect consumers, protect the worker–"are all approaches to political control and absolute tyranny."[5]

Take wage and price controls, for example. They are instituted by government to divert blame for rising prices away from government, which is destroying the currency, toward the business sector. Unjust? Of course it is. Wage and price controls are totally incompatible with a free system because 1) they are by definition arbitrary, and 2) it is impossible to impose them without interfering with the functions of the marketplace. Wage and price controls prohibit the function of the price mechanism that brings supply and demand together. The outcome is shortages, shoddy products, and finally goods disappearing from the market. They may be cheap, but there "ain't none." The end result of "distributive justice" will not be a modification of the existing marketplace, "but its complete abandonment and its replacement by an altogether different system–the command economy."[6]

A perfect example is the history of the oil and gas industry. Under controls since 1954, the price of natural gas was kept artificially low by the Federal Power Commission. Therefore, homeowners and businesses consumed cheap natural gas in prodigious amounts for decades. By the 1970s, however, the cheap price left the market undersupplied and shortages began to develop. The FPC, frightened by this situation, started lifting the ceiling to allow the price to rise a little. The net effect is that historically the price of natural gas is cheap. But some communities, businesses, and states, who have grown dependent on the cheap fuel, are finding out there "ain't none." (For a full discussion on the government-created "energy crisis," the reader is referred to the author's previous book *Gold and Black Gold.*)

Jefferson put it succinctly when he remarked, "Agriculture, Manufactures, Commerce, and Navigation, the four Pillars of our Prosperity, are the most thriving when left to individual Enterprise."

In an article entitled "The Assault on Integrity," Alan Greenspan explains the true motives and effects of government regulation.

"Government regulation is not an alternative means of protecting the consumer," says Greenspan. "It does not build quality into goods, or accuracy into information. Its sole 'contribution' is to substitute force and fear for incentive as the 'protector' of the consumer.... At the bottom of the endless pile of paper work which characterizes all regulation lies a gun."

The result is predictable, for bad "protection" drives out good protection, to paraphrase Gresham's Law. "The attempt to protect the consumer by force undercuts the protection he gets from incentive. First, it undercuts the value of reputation by placing the reputable company on the same basis as the unknown, the newcomer, or fly-by-nighter. It declares, in effect, that all are equally suspect and that years of evidence to the contrary do not free a man from that suspicion. Second, it grants an automatic (though, in fact, unachievable) guarantee of safety to the products of any company that complies with its arbitrarily set minimum standards. The value of a reputation rested on the fact that it was necessary for the consumers to exercise judgment in the choice of the goods and services they purchased. The government's 'guarantee' undermines this necessity; it declares to the consumers, in effect, that no choice or judgment is required—and that a company's record, its years of achievement, is irrelevant."

In short, the responsibility is lifted from both the consumer and the producer. Freedom requires responsibility; without one the other is non-existent. "The guiding purpose of the government regulator is to prevent rather than to create something," asserts Greenspan. That is why agencies like the Food and Drug Administration would rather ban all new drugs than be guilty of allowing one harmful one to escape detection. Consequently, very few new drugs reach the market and those that do are very costly. Many drugs now available in Canada, Mexico, and Europe are prohibited in the United States. The individual is not even allowed to choose, to take a chance on life rather than death.

"Protection of the consumer by regulation is thus illusory," reports Greenspan. "Rather than isolating the consumer from the dishonest businessman, it is gradually destroying the only reliable protection the consumer has: competition for reputation.... Moreover, 'protective' legislation falls in the category of preventive law. Businessmen are being subjected to government coercion *prior* to the commission of any crime." For instance, Monroe H. Freedman, Dean of Hofstra University School of Law, confirms that "open violations of basic rights and outright intimidation of individuals, business firms and attorneys through aggressive abuse of its powers are common S.E.C.

[Security & Exchange Commission] tactics." (*National Enterprise*, December 10, 1975.)

The free enterprise system is based on man's self-interest and self-esteem. "It holds integrity and trustworthiness as cardinal virtues and makes them pay off in the market place, thus demanding that men survive by means of virtues, not of vices,"[7] This is a superlatively moral and just system.

The issue is not between pro-business and pro-consumer, but between regulations and freedom. Government regulations and controls of the economy, no matter in whose behalf, have been the source of all the evils in our economic history. Government regulations, sometimes called "planning," simply yields poor and inefficient government agencies and inefficient and costly businesses. One can plan for slavery, but one cannot plan for free-enterprise, for freedom.

The attitude of government toward business is even destructive, as the president of Fruehauf Corp. reports: "I would rather walk in with a problem to the Kremlin than I would to the Federal Trade Commission." The F.T.C. feels "all business is bad.... I have never seen a group of people so anti-business." (*L.A. Times*, September 6, 1974)

What has all this government protection cost the businessman and the consumer? Walton reports these astounding figures: It costs $20 billion a year to handle the paper work involved with government regulations. Another $20 billion a year to pay for government printers, processors, and papershufflers. "*That's $40 billion a year for red tape, triplicate forms, filing cabinets, postage stamps and wastepaper baskets*."[8] And it is *all* counter-productive.

For example, Walton cites the 1,100 different permits and approvals required before construction of the Alaskan pipeline could begin. The original cost estimate was $1 billion. It is no wonder that after years of political demagoguery and government regulation, the actual cost came to over $6 billion, which is, of course, a large part of the high price of gasoline.

Another example is the Civil Aeronautics Board. It has imposed "excess fares" and "excess capacity" regulations, which have cost air passengers more than $100 million in 1969 alone.[9] Louis A. Engman, chairman of the Federal Trade Commission had the nerve to admit that regulations of business amount to little more than "government sanctioned price fixing." (*L.A. Times*, October 8, 1974)

A final example is that of the new agency, the Federal Energy Administration (F.E.A.). When the F.E.A. went into business, the United States was importing about one third of its oil. In only *three* years, the F.E.A. has grown from nothing to 3,400 of the highest paid government employees; the mean salary of F.E.A. employees is $19,000. More than 110 of these employees are public relations experts cranking out 60 press releases a month and costing taxpapers more than $3 million a year.

The F.E.A. has also managed to increase our imports to fifty percent a year. (*Access to Energy*, July 1, 1976)

In total, the cost of government has been growing at a rate of eleven percent per year while personal income has been rising at a rate of eight percent a year. The average cost of government in 1974 amounted to $2,146 for every man, woman, and child. If figured solely on the basis of each producer–each man and woman in the labor force, it amounted to $5,290. There are now fifty percent of the labor force working on the public (government) payroll and fifty percent in the private sector, supporting the public sector. How long can this last and when will the producers revolt? That is the big question.

In 1913, before the days of paternalistic government, the percentage of total personal income to total government spending was 9.5 percent. The estimated figure for 1974 is 43.1 percent.[10] That is, nearly one-half of all income is going to support the government payroll, and it is rising. This does not count the "hidden taxes." To add insult to injury, Walton cites a recent survey that shows the rate of productivity per man-hour in government is *thirty-nine percent below* the average productivity level of the private sector.[11]

Walton supplies us with two conclusions. One, while government is so busy shuffling paper and interfering in (destroying) other people's business, its responsibilities of law, order and justice have fallen by the board. Second, he quotes the noted British archeologist, Sir Flinders Petrie, who studied the records of the world's six great civilizations of the past 8,000 years, and concluded, "When economic 'parasitism' sets in–when government and its allies of the special interest factions feast on the fruits of the working man's labor–civilizations slide into the abyss or a prolonged 'dark ages.' And, few recover."[12]

What is the solution? Repeal *all* regulations on business–free the businessman, allow him and/or make him compete for the consumers' dollars. Second, abolish the hundreds of federal advisory boards, committees, commissions, and councils. Here lies the waste and boondoggles; here is where to cut government spending. The "Fifth arm" of government is staffed by more than 4,000 government employees and 24,000 private citizens. There are committees for everything from anti-perspirants to anthropology, nearly 12,000 of them, or one committee for every 18,000 Americans.[13]

There is a saying that "nothing comes closer to achieving immortality [or is it immorality] than a federal program." But what Congress has created, it can repeal. There is nothing sacred about a government program.

In closing, here are some words of wisdom by Adam Smith: "The statesman who should attempt to direct private people in what manner they ought to employ their capitals, would not only load himself with a most unnecessary attention, but assume an authority which could safely be trusted to no council and senate whatever, and which would nowhere be so dangerous as in the hands of a man who had folly and presumption enough to fancy himself fit to exercise it."

NOTES ON REGULATIONS, CHAPTER XIV

1. *Conceived in Liberty*, Vol. I, Pp. 505-06.
2. *Conceived in Liberty*, Vol. III, P. 280.
3. New York: Crown Publishers, 1947, P. 231, quoted in *Capitalism: The Unknown Ideal.*
4. *Capitalism: The Unknown Ideal*, Pp. 96-102.
5. *God of the Machine*, P. 184.
6. *Constitution of Liberty*, P. 232.
7. *Capitalism: The Unknown Ideal*, Pp. 113-16.
8. Op. Cit., P. 154.
9. IBID., P. 155.
10. IBID., Pp. 202-03.
11. IBID., P. 198.
12. IBID., P. 219.
13. Donald Lambro, *The Federal Rathole*, (New Rochelle, New York: Arlington House, 1975), P. 23.

XV

Money, Debt, Legal Tender, Central Banking

Whenever destroyers appear among men, they start by destroying money, for money is men's protection and the base of a moral existence. Destroyers seize gold and leave to its owners a counterfeit pile of paper. This kills all objective standards and delivers men into the arbitrary power of an arbitrary setter of values. Gold was an objective value, an equivalent of wealth produced. Paper is a mortgage on wealth that does not exist, backed by a gun aimed at those who are expected to produce it. Paper is a check drawn by legal looters upon an account which is not theirs: upon the virtue of the victims.

AYN RAND,
ATLAS SHRUGGED

The purpose of this chapter is to point out the evils committed and harm done when government monopolizes the money and credit supplies. Injustice reigns supreme when government becomes the banker for the nation.

Governments monopolize the money supply because of the power it yields. It allows government to create money at will, set the value of the currency, profit by printing a certain dollar amount on a piece of paper and then spend it at that value, create credit, set interest rates, and, in short, control the country.

What is money? Money is some thing of lasting value that men keep in exchange for goods and services, to be spent at a later date for the perishable supports of life. Money was an invention of man as trade progressed. It is worth only what it can buy. As a medium of exchange it holds no intrinsic value, unless it is a commodity such as gold or silver—the intrinsic value being the market price of the metal. Money allows a man to possess more than he can make use of immediately, so that he can save and plan.

Money also possesses a moral basis: Money is created by men working voluntarily to produce something of value to trade one another. Free trade allows deals of mutual consent and benefit without force or coercion. It rewards the best in man. It is a symbol of his highest ability. Without money the force of a gun prevails (as in Russia), a double standard arises, and legalized theft appears. Thus money is the barometer of a society. Evil men try to destroy money's objective value by seizing gold and substituting paper.

Americans were the first to recognize the justice of "making money." They were the first to recognize that money had to be made before it can be confiscated and redistributed. The phrase "to make money" contains the essence of morality. In short, money is the root of all good.[1] Your own destruction, dear reader, follows upon any other premise.

Today we use paper for money; our gold was confiscated in 1933. In 1968 the remaining gold backing behind the dollar was removed by Congress. Our currency is worth whatever our government says its worth. And our government is depreciating the value of it by printing more and more at will. Inflation, as it is commonly called, is truly currency depreciation. There is only one solution, to back the currency again with something of value, i.e., gold–the Gold Standard is the only proven way to keep a currency valuable. (For a complete explanation of the virtues of the Gold Standard the reader is referred to the author's book *Why Gold?*)

The American Revolutionary era saw an abundance of literature on the subject of money. Americans had learned the hard way, firsthand from the war, the effects of depreciating currency. The debates on hard money versus paper raged throughout the colonies (after the plague of the worthless Continentals), until the issue was supposedly settled by the Constitution. The verdict was in favor of *hard* money: Article, I, Section 10 states: "No state shall....make anything but gold and silver coin a tender in payment of debts."

Number 44 of *The Federalist*, written by Madison, succinctly summarized the Founding Fathers reasons for trusting only gold and silver money: Prohibiting paper money "must give pleasure to every citizen, in proportion to his love of justice and his knowledge of the true springs of public prosperity. The loss which America has sustained since the peace from the pestilent effects of paper money on the necessary confidence between man and man...on the industry and morals of the people and on the character of republican government, constitutes an enormous debt against the States chargable with this unadvised measure, which must long remain unsatisfied; or rather an accumulation of guilt, which can be expiated no otherwise than by a voluntary sacrifice on the altar of justice of the power which has been the instrument of it."

The argument *for paper money* is that it is cheaper to borrow because interest rates are artificially lowered, and it is easier to repay loans while there is an abundance of paper money in circulation. The argument *for hard money* is simply that is requires a loan to be paid back in the same value of money by which it was lent. Only the latter is just. If the discussion centered around justice–right and wrong–the issue could be settled forthwith. Otherwise, there is no solution. Those in power will work it out to their best advantage, and justice be damned.

In "A Collection of Essays and Fugitive Writings" in 1790, Noah Webster wrote about legal tender laws. Such laws force all to accept worthless paper as a tender in payment of debts. Webster declared:

> ...a tender law is the devil. When I trust a man a sum of money, I expect he will return the full value. That legislature which says my debtor may pay me with one-third of the value he received commits a deliberate act of villainy; an act for which an individual, in any government, would be honored with a whipping-post, and in most governments, with a gallows. ...
>
> But legislatures can, with the solemn face of rulers and guardians of justice, boldly give currency to an adultered coin, enjoin it upon debtors to cheat their creditors, and enforce their systematic knavery with legal penalties. The difference between the man who makes and passes countefeit money, and the man who tenders his creditor one-third of the value of the debt and demands a discharge, is the same as between a thief and a robber.
>
> My countrymen, the devil is among you. Remember that past contracts are sacred things; that legislatures have no right to interfere with them; they have no right to say a debt shall be paid at a discount, or in any manner which the parties never intended. It is the business of justice to fulfill the intention of parties in contracts, not to defeat them. To pay bona fide contracts for cash, in paper of little value, or in old horses, would be a dishonest attempt in an individual; but for legislatures to frame laws to support and encourage such detestable villainy is like a judge who should inscribe the arms of a rogue over the seat of justice....
>
> My countrymen, I am a private, peaceable man. I have nothing to win or to lose by the game of paper currency; but I revere justice. I would sooner pick

> oakum all my life than stain my reputation, or pay my creditors one farthing less than his honest demands.
>
> But when...legislatures make paper or old horses a legal tender in all cases, the world will exclaim with one voice, Ye are rogues, and the devil is in you!"[2]

Today the currency of the United States is legal tender, as noted in the upper left-hand corner of any Federal Reserve Note. These notes were declared legal tender in 1933 by government edict. Another act by government edict (and in contempt of the Constitution) removed the gold behind them.

Legal tender laws allow debtors to repay loans at discounted rates, while creditors receive money that buys less each year. This is clearly unjust. But legal tender laws *force* a creditor to accept a depreciating currency.

Currency depreciation and legal tender laws are more than issues between debtors and creditors. They are propositions by which everyone in society loses. They are also clearly unconstitutional. As Chief Justice Salmon P. Chase quoted Daniel Webster: " there is no legal tender...under the authority of this government....This is a constitutional principle perfectly plain and of the very highest importance. The States are prohibited from making anything but gold and silver a tender in payment of debts, and although no such express prohibition is applied to Congress, *yet as Congress has no power granted to it in this respect but to coin money and regulate the value of foreign coin,* it clearly has no power to substitute paper or anything else for coin as a tender in payment of debts and in discharge of contracts."[3]

By declaring our money legal tender the government has usurped the citizen's right of choosing his money. It did so in order to protect a currency which would eventually become worthless. Legal tender laws go hand in hand with inflation. As government depreciates the currency, individuals start looking for protection. Before the Gold Standard and Gold Clauses in contracts were outlawed, the people could turn to gold for payment. But a government intent on destroying a currency cannot leave an avenue of escape. Thus, it forces the holders of the currency to use that currency exclusively and prohibits any competing commodity. In short, it creates a monopoly.

The Founding Fathers absolutely abhorred the use of currency depreciation and tender laws, wanted nothing whatsoever to do with them, and held in contempt anyone so base and so evil as to suggest their usage.

During the Revolution, for example, Henry wrote to Richard Henry Lee, "In my opinion, these miscreants who forge our money are much more criminal than most other offenders, as parricide exceeds murder.... I believe most nations have agreed in considering and punishing the contamination of money as the highest crimes against society are considered and punished.... The loss of our liberty seems at present more likely to be derived from the state of our currency than from all other sources." Further on Henry lays the greatest source of danger to the "consequent corruption of morals among the people." Finally, Virginia voted against paper emissions because "an emission of paper currency would be ruinous to trade and commerce, and highly injurious to the good people of this Commonwealth."

It is a toss-up between Paine and Jefferson for who wrote more about the evils of paper money. Both vehemently denounced them along with their protectors, tender laws and central banking. Because of their thoroughness, Paine's writings will be quoted at length from Volumes IV and V of the *Life and Works of Thomas Paine.*

Paine begins with a simple statement: "Money is money, and paper is paper." He continues:

> All the invention of man cannot make them otherwise. Gold and silver are emissions of nature: paper is the emission of art. The value of gold and silver is ascertained by the quantity which nature has made in the earth....Therefore the value being dependent upon the quantity, depends not on man.
>
> Its being stamped into coin adds considerably to its convenience but nothing to its value. It has then no more value than it had before. Its value is not in the impression but in itself. Take away the impression and still the same value remains. Alter it as you will, or expose it to any misfortune that can happen, still the value is not diminished. It has a capacity to resist the accidents that destroy other things. It has, therefore, all the requisite qualities that money can have, and is a fit material to make money of; and nothing which has not all those properties, can be fit for the purpose of money.
>
> The only proper use for paper, in the room of money, is to write promissory notes and obligations of payment in specie upon. A piece of paper, thus written and signed, is worth the sum it is given for, if the person who gives it is able to pay it; because in this case, the law will oblige him. But if he is worth nothing, the paper note is worth nothing.
>
> But when an assembly undertake to issue paper *as* money, the whole system of safety and certainty is overturned, and property set afloat. Money, when considered as the fruit of many year's industry, as the reward of labor, sweat and toil, as the widow's dowry and children's portion, and as the means of procuring

the necessaries and alleviating the afflictions of life, and making old age a scene of rest, has something in it sacred that is not to be sported with, or trusted to the airy bubble of paper currency.

By what power or authority an assembly undertakes to make paper money, is difficult to say. It derives none from the Constitution, for that is silent on the subject. It is one of those things which the people have not delegated, and which, were they at any time assembled together, they would not delegate. It is, therefore, an assumption of power which an assembly is not warranted in, and which may, one day or other, be the means of bringing some of them to punishment.

One of the evils of paper money is, that it turns the whole country into stock jobbers. The precariousness of its value and the uncertainty of its fate continually operate, night and day, to produce this destructive effect. Having no real value in itself it depends for support upon accident, caprice and party, and as it is the interest of some to depreciate and of others to raise its value, there is a continual invention going on that destroys the morals of the country.

The pretense for paper money has been, that there was not sufficiency of gold and silver. This, so far from being a reason for emissions, is a reason against them.

As to the assumed authority of any assembly in making paper money, or paper of any kind, a legal tender, or in other language, a compulsive payment, it is a most presumptuous attempt at arbitrary power. There can be no such power in a republican government: the people have no freedom, and property no security where this practice can be acted: and the committee who shall bring in a report for this purpose, or the member who moves for it, and he who seconds it merits impeachment, and sooner or later may expect it.

Of all the various sorts of base coin, paper money is the basest. It has the least intrinsic value of anything that can be put in the place of gold and silver. A hobnail or a piece of wampum far exceeds it. And there would be more propriety in making those articles a legal tender than to make paper so.

The laws of a country ought to be the standard of equity, and calculated to impress on the minds of the people the moral as well as the legal obligations of reciprocal justice. But tender laws, of any kind, operate to destroy morality, and to dissolve, by the pretense of law, what ought to be the principle of law to support, reciprocal justice between man and man: and the punishment of a member who should move for such a law ought to be *death*.

Tender laws continue to be the means of fraud.

If anything had, or could have, a value equal to gold and silver, it would require no tender law: and if it had not that value it ought not to have such a law; and, therefore, all tender laws are tyrannical and unjust, and calculated to support fraud and oppression.

Most of the advocates for tender laws are those who have debts to discharge, and who take refuge in such a law, to violate their contracts and cheat their creditors... every idea of tender laws [ought to be] publicly reprobated and extirpated from among us.

As to paper money, in any light it can be viewed, it is at best a bubble. Considered as property, it is inconsistent to suppose that the breath of an assembly, whose authority expires with the year, can give to paper the value and duration of gold.... And by the precedent, (for authority there is none,) that one assembly makes paper money, another may do the same, until confidence and credit are totally expelled, and all the evils of depreciation acted over again. The amount, therefore, of paper money is this, that it is the illegimate offspring of assemblies, and when their year expires, they leave a vagrant on the hands of the public.

[When a central bank acts as government's banker,] this is the connection that threatens to ruin every public bank. It is through this connection that the credit of a bank is forced far beyond what it ought to be, and still further beyond its ability to pay. It is through this connection that such an immense redundant quantity of bank notes have gotten into circulation; and which, instead of being issued because there was property in the bank, have been issued because there was none. The central bank acts not only as an ordinary bank, but as a great engine of state.

Before the invention of paper money (bank notes), there was no other money in the nation than gold and silver, and the greatest quantity of money that was ever raised in taxes during that period never exceeded a fourth part of the quantity of money in the nation.

> To go beyond this limit of a fourth part...they were obliged to introduce paper money.
>
> It is worthy of observation that every case of failure in finances, since the system of paper began, has produced a revolution in governments, either total or partial."

That is the story of paper money, central banks and legal tender laws. All are unjust, fraudulent and destructive. Jefferson's writings agreed with Paine's. On finance, Jefferson believed "the accounts of the United States ought to be, and may be, made as simple as those of a common farmer, and capable of being understood by common farmers." He further believed that the doctrine of perpetual debt is inadmissable, for no generation has a right to lay a tribute for its wars and extravagances upon posterity.

"No man is more ardently intent to see the public debt soon and sacredly paid off than I am," said Jefferson."I place economy among the first and most important of republican virtues, and public debt as the greatest of the dangers to be feared." He added that "it is a wise rule and should be fundamental in a government disposed to cherish its credit, and at the same time to restrain the use of it within the limits of its faculties, never to borrow a dollar without laying a tax in the same instant for paying the interest annually and the principal within a given time."

On paper money, or the promise of something for nothing, Jefferson had this to say: "We are now taught to believe that legerdemain tricks upon paper can produce as solid wealth as hard labor on the earth. It is vain for common sense to urge that *nothing* can produce but *nothing*: that it is an idle dream to believe in a philosopher's stone which is to turn everything into gold, and to redeem man from the original sentence of his maker, 'in the sweat of his brow shall he eat his bread.' "

Jefferson fought all attempts of the paper-money men to push ahead their schemes. He called them "monocrats" and "paper men," who wanted armies and debts, to enable them to get offices or jobs for themselves or friends.

Always an advocate of hard money, Jefferson believed that government should maintain a metallic currency which will preserve its own level, and "can never die in our hands.... the trifling economy of paper as a cheaper medium, or its convenience for transmission, weighs nothing in opposition to the advantages of the precious metals. An inconvertible paper currency is not only liable to be abused, but always has been and always will be abused in every country where it is permitted."

If all these passages seem tiring to the reader, please bear with me, for this is the most important chapter in the entire book; this is where freedom and justice are established for all, or for only a few (tyranny). This is the foundation of all good government.

Regarding the unconstitutionality of a central bank, Jefferson astutely called Hamilton's scheme "calculated to undermine and demolish the republic." It "flowed from principles adverse to liberty," and would create a moneyed interest that would have power over the government and the people by placing government in debt to it through the bank. (And it certainly has; today the interest on the national debt is the third largest item on the federal budget and growing rapidly.) Jefferson based his opinion of the unconstitutionality of the proposed central bank on the Twelfth Amendment, and to take a single step beyond a constitutional boundary is to enter a never-never land of no limits. He staunchly believed that the Constitution was intended to lace Congress up straitly within the enumerated powers.

(A special bureau in the Treasury Department spent $114 million in 1977 just to keep track of the public debt. Arthur Andersen & Co., one of the country's largest CPA firms, reported that if corporations kept track of their costs and revenues the way the government does, company officers would be hauled off to jail or the firms would end in bankruptcy.)

How is this chicanery achieved? Jefferson explained that Hamilton, the first Secretary of the Treasury, was able to so complicate the banking system that neither he nor Congress could unravel it. And "while he was giving himself the airs of providing for the payment of the debt, he left himself free to add to it continually, as he did in fact, instead of paying it." Today, the Federal Reserve does not even try to pay off the debt; it makes no pretense that it is continually adding to it.

The running and ruining of a country by a central bank has been the way of things in Europe for hundreds of years. The first two central banks in the United States failed to take hold because the people were too wise to tolerate such a predatorial institution. In a letter to John Taylor on May 28, 1816, Jefferson wrote these famous lines: "And I sincerely believe, with you, that banking establishments are more dangerous than standing armies; and that the principle of spending money to be paid by posterity, under the name of funding, is but swindling futurity on a large scale."[4]

In essence, Jefferson believed that a nation's banking system should be separate from its government. He considered the central bank an institution of "the most deadly hostility...against the principles and form of our Constitution...."

When Andrew Jackson vetoed the charter for the establishment of the Second Bank of the United States on July 10, 1832 he sent a message to Congress listing his reasons. We can do no less than study excerpts from this worthy and brilliant document, which defined the Jacksonian Era as the defender of the common man, not the privileged few:

> The powers and privileges possessed by the existing bank are unauthorized by the Constitution, subversive of the rights of the states, and dangerous to the liberties of the people.... I can perceive none of those modifications of the bank charter which are necessary, in my opinion, to make it compatible with justice, with sound policy, or with the Constitution of our country.
>
> Every monopoly and all exclusive privileges are granted at the expense of the public.
>
> It is regretted that the rich and powerful too often bend the acts of government to their selfish purposes.... There are no necessary evils in government. Its evils exist only in its abuses. If it would confine itself to equal protection, it would be an unqualified blessing. In the act before me there seems to be a wide and unnecessary departure from these just principles.
>
> Most of the difficulties our government now encounters and most of the dangers which impend over our Union have sprung from an abandonment of the legitimate objects of government by our national legislation and the adoption of such principles as are embodied in this act....We have in the results of our legislation arrayed section against section, interest against interest, and man against man, in a fearful commotion which threatens to shake the foundations of our Union.
>
> It is time to pause in our career to review our principles and, if possible, revive that devoted patriotism and spirit of...the sages of the Revolution and fathers of our Union.... We can at least take a stand against all new grants of monopolies and exclusive privileges, against any prostitution of our government to the advancement of the few at the expense of the many...."[5]

It is imperative that we, too, rethink fundamental principles, for the time has come to either change our way of life and our institutions (the Federal Reserve System, Internal Revenue Service, etc.) or continue to suffer the consequences, which will assuredly worsen. Herein lies the great benefits of reading, studying and enacting the lessons of history.

In defense of honesty and integrity as opposed to a central bank, the *Niles' Weekly Register* on May 9, 1818 published the following article:

> Whenever a state of public feeling is produced, where men are not ashamed of being in debt, the mind loses its proper sense of manly independence; and whenever the salutary obstacles to borrowing money are removed, and men are *invited* to become debtors by the facility of borrowing, the axe is laid to the root of national industry, which is the foundation of national virtue and prosperity. In no well-organized state of society ought the generality of men to become borrowers, and in no class of any community can borrowing become general, without ultimately ending in its ruin....
>
> There *was* a time...when it was disgraceful in a farmer to borrow money, and his respectability was seriously injured by becoming a dependent on banks. These honest people...saw that the art of becoming rich, without either capital or industry–the power of creating wealth from *rags*–must, in the end, inevitably prove highly injurious to every man possessed of real property. It was plain that if men could grow rich by such means, the value of industry and land must continue to diminish insensibly, because it is impossible to give a fictitious value to any imaginary and worthless commodity without diminishing, in the like proportion, the value of what is real.
>
> The farmer... saw and felt that the system of rags must either be destroyed or that he must become an accomplice or a victim."[6]

In short, the practice of going into debt instead of living within one's means tends to make people believe they can get away with something–cheat reality. Thus they are corrupted, along with the banking system that creates loans out of thin air and then collects interest on the money, too.

Money is one of the greatest instruments of freedom ever invented by man. A sound currency is so crucial that John M. Keynes once remarked, "There is no subtler, no surer means of overturning the existing basis of society than to debauch the currency." Similarly, Lenin said, "The best way to destroy the capitalist system was to debauch the currency." Indeed, Keynes admitted that the individualistic free-enterprise system of today, "precisely because it entrusts saving to the individual investor and production to the individual employer, *presumes* a stable measuring-rod of values, and cannot be efficient–perhaps, cannot survive–without one."[7]

That is the bottom line, the truth. And central banks, national debts, depreciating currencies, and legal tender laws spell one thing–the end of free enterprise, freedom and justice. Jefferson claimed,

"Banks, by their easy paper issues, seduced ambitious farmers from the labors of the plow into careers of gambling and speculation, then to save their own skins bankrupted the farms." The net result of inflation and national debt is economic collapse, depression, and finally rebellion. (This was illustrated in the discussion on the French Revolution. In the wake of the French Revolution was misery, poverty, depression, and despair, paving the road for a dictator, who promised relief. Napolean promised and delivered relief by restoring gold to the currency. He brought stability back to France. He was then able to go on to conquer most of Europe.)

Jefferson and Paine were not economists; there were none then, for things were simple and understandable. It is only in recent history that people are at a loss to understand our extremely complex and complicated public financial systems. That in itself should be a warning that something is amiss. There is only one reason to hide the truth; that is, to bury the misdeeds of legislatures under mounds of laws, rules, institutions, and a horrendous national debt of *over $7 trillion* and climbing.

In a letter to Samuel Kercheval, dated July 12, 1816, Jefferson sums up the heretofore mentioned evils:

> And to preserve their independence, we must not let our rulers load us with perpetual debt. We must make our election between *economy and liberty* [note how the definition of economy, where it used to mean frugality, today has been perverted to mean the state of the nation's economic system], or *profusion and servitude*. If we run into such debts, as that we must be taxed in our meat and in our drink, in our necessaries and our comforts, in our labors and our amusements, for our callings and our creeds, as the people of England are, our people, like them, must come to labor sixteen hours in the twenty-four, give the earnings of fifteen of these to the government for their debts and daily expenses; and the sixteenth being insuffucient to afford us bread, we must live, as they now do, on oatmeal and potatoes, have no time to think, no means of calling the mismanagers to account; but be glad to obtain subsistence by hiring ourselves to rivet their chains on the necks of our fellow sufferers....
>
> A departure from principle in one instance becomes a precedent for a second; that second, for a third; and so on, till the bulk of the society is reduced to be mere automatons of misery, to have no sensibilities left but for serving and sinning. Then begins, indeed, the *bellum omnium in omnia* [war of all against all].... And the fore horse of this frightful team is public debt. Taxation

> follows that, and, in its train, wretchedness and oppression."[8]

The decision Americans now must make is to abolish the Federal Reserve System, legal tender laws, the Internal Revenue Service, and to set up a Gold Standard and a schedule to pay off the national debt, to redeem our independence. The choice, you say, is impracticable. Is the alternative of slavery, bankruptcy, poverty and dictatorship preferrable? In short, there really is no choice; politics got us into this mess, it can get us out.

Mention of the efficaciousness of the Gold Standard has been omitted since it has been covered in the author's previous book, *Why Gold?*, but we would like to include here short excerpts from a speech by William Bourke Cockran, who on August 18, 1896, appeared in Madison Square Garden to reply to William Jennings Bryan's famous "cross of gold" speech. Earlier Cockran, an orator-statesman and eminent democrat from Ireland, had proclaimed, "The movement launched in Chicago is an attempt to paralyze industry by using all the powers of government to take property from the hands of those who created it and place it in the hands of those who covet it." Here is his defense of the Gold Standard:

> [Stripped of all verbal disguises, eliminating the Gold Standard] is an issue of *common honesty,* an issue between the *honest discharge* and the *dishonest repudiation* of *public and private obligations*. It is a question as to whether the powers of government shall be used to protect honest industry or to tempt the citizen to dishonesty.
>
> On this question *honest men cannot differ*. It is one of *morals and justice*. It involves the existence of social order. It is the contest of civilization itself.... Democratic leaders...cannot seduce the footsteps of Democratic voters from the pathway of honor and justice....
>
> It will prove that the American people cannot be divided into parties on a question of simple morals or of common honesty....
>
> Nothing is more common than the mistake that money and property are identical. They are not. A redundancy of money does not prove any prosperity. There may be a very large amount of circulating medium and very great poverty. The issue of paper money simply is no more an increase of wealth than the issue by an individual of his promissory note would show an increase of his property.

> [You shall not rob the American working man] of any one advantage which he has gained by long years of study, of progress in the skill of his craft....You shall not obscure the golden prospect of a further improvement in his condition by a further appreciation of the cost of living as well as by a further cheapening of the dollar which is paid to him.
>
> There can be no distress, there can be no hard times, when labor is well paid....The time has come when the people of this country will show their capacity for self-government. They will prove that the men who have led the world in the pathway of progress will be the jealous guardians of liberty and honor. They are not to be seduced by appeals to their cupidity or moved by threats of injury.... When...this *assault upon common honesty* and upon industry, shall have abated forever...The government will still shelter a people indissolubly wedded to liberty and order, jealously forbidding any distinction of burden or of privilege, conserving property, maintaining morality, resting forever upon the broad basis of American patriotism and American intelligence.'"[9] (Emphasis added.)

(With Cockran's backing, McKinley, a Republican, trounced Bryan by a popular majority of six hundred thousand votes.) On March 14, 1900, the United States officially adopted the Gold Standard, when the dollar became the "the standard unit of value," of twenty-five and four-fifths grains of ninety percent fine gold. However, the United States repealed the Gold Standard in 1933, rekindling the fires of inflation. The reply of Senator Carter Glass upon hearing such a dastardly deed was: "It's dishonor, Sir. This great Government....is breaking its promise to redeem its paper money in gold coin of the present standard of value. It's dishonor, Sir."

The following is a poem entitled "The Gold Dollar," by E. Mason, which sums up eloquently and nobly the argument for sound, 'hard money:

Ah, little gold dollar, republican name
Let peace be thy motto, and freedom thy fame;
May all use thee kindly and not hide thy face
Like misers and bankers in some lonely place,
But gain thee by labor or calling that's just,
And part with thee freely whenever they must;
Let laborers adore thee as both king and civil
Though bankers may make thee the root of all evil.

'Twas labor that caus'd thee to leave the gold mine
'Twas labor that made thee in splendor to shine,
'Twas labor that coin'd thee and fashion'd the mold
To shape thee so nicely a dollar of gold.
Since dollars and labor are nearly allied
In payment for labor they should be applied;
And all who will labor six days out of seven,
Gold dollars in payment should always be given.

'Tis cheating of labors when misers do hold
And store up so useless those dollars of gold;
'Tis knavery that bankers should keep them in bags,
And substitute for thee a vile trash of rags;
A bill made of paper, pure gold to alloy,
To build up the rich and the poor to destroy.
Unknown to our fathers who fought for our freedom,
Forbid it ye younger who now doth succeed them.

Arise then ye freemen, use liberty's hand
And drive this vile paper from liberty's land,
And let the gold dollar be coin for the poor
And circulate freely to every man's door.
Awake up to freedom and be not controll'd,
Submit not to bankers to pocket your gold.
Put down the whole system of legalized knaving
And down with the brokers who now live by shaving.

Now look about the country and see those that shirk
Too idle to labor, too lazy to work,
Bank bills are their hobby, they live at their ease,
And make a new issue whenever they please;
They sport on the inter'st of bills they have lent,
Whose capital value is not worth a cent.

And cheating so common, the nicest inspector
Is forced to keep by him a bank note detector.

Then freemen use wisdom, be free when you can,
Drive all the small paper from liberty's land,
Send back to the bankers all notes under tens,
And draw back the specie to make you amends;
And henceforth refusing this paper disgrace,
Gold dollars and silver will soon take their place.
Our country will stand on a footing more civil,
And freemen rejoice at the down fall of evil.

In conclusion, Jefferson's words of wisdom speak to us again: "Everything predicted by the enemies of banks, in the beginning is now coming to pass. We are to be ruined now by the deluge of bank paper, as we were formerly by the old Continental paper. It is cruel that such revolutions in private fortunes should be at the mercy of avaricious adventurers, who instead of employing their capital, if any they have, in manufactures, commerce and other useful pursuits, make it an instrument to burden all the interchanges of property with their swindling profits which are the price of no useful industry of theirs. Prudent men must be on their guard in this game of *Robin's alive,* and take care that the spark does not extinguish in their hands. I am an enemy to all banks discounting bills or notes for anything but coin." (Letter to Dr. Thomas Cooper, January 16, 1814.)

NOTES ON MONEY, DEBT, LEGAL TENDER, CENTRAL BANKING, CHAPTER XV

1. *Atlas Shrugged*, Pp. 410-15.
2. *Annals of America*, Vol. 3, Pp. 67-68.
3. As quoted by Howard S. Katz, *The Paper Aristocracy*, (New York: Books in Focus, Inc., 1976), P. 71.
4. *Annals of America*, Vol. 4, P. 418.
5. IBID., Vol. 5, Pp. 524-535.
6. IBID., Vol. 4, P. 501.
7. *Constitution of Liberty*, P. 520.
8. *Annals of America*, Vol. 4, Pp. 424-25.
9. *A Treasury of the World's Great Speeches*, Pp. 642-48.

XVI

Taxation

One must wait for the time when the nation [U.S.A.] will have recourse to conscription and to heavy taxes to be able to judge what sacrifies democracies can impose on themselves.
ALEXIS DE TOCQUEVILLE

Steadily increasing taxation is placing American citizens dangerously close to bondage.
CONGRESSMAN PHILIP CRANE, ILLINOIS, 1975

Webster's dictionary says a tax is a "rate imposed on property or persons for the benefit of the state." Most people agree on what taxes are. Most agree that they are necessary for the support of the government. But how much? A problem arises when taxation becomes excessive and oppressive. It is here that individuals become polarized, depending upon whether they are on the paying end or the receiving end of the taxes. What is fair?

Montesquieu defines the public revenue as that portion that "each subject gives of his property, in order to secure or enjoy the remainder." He warns that the real wants of the people ought never to give way to the imaginary wants of the state. Taxation should not be measured by the people's abilities to give, but by what they ought to give,[1] because the effect of wealth in a country should inspire every heart with ambition, while that of poverty should give birth to despair. The former is brought about by fairly taxed labor, the latter is established by oppressive taxation, which deprives people of the fruits of their labor, leaving them discontent at their work.

Montesquieu points out that the natural tax of moderate governments is the sales tax. Laid on merchandise it is "more natural to liberty, by reason it has not so direct a relation to the person." A capitation or income tax is "more natural to slavery." Trouble arises when a moderate government, which has been successful in collecting taxes, lays moderation aside to carry taxation to excess. Liberty, which produced the available taxes in the first place, is overlooked, thus producing slavery, which is the effect of excessive taxation. And the net effect of slavery produces a diminution of taxes.

Rousseau observed that income taxes and sales taxes on the necessaries of life, as they directly trespass on the right of property, are always liable to have dangerous results. Wise governments prudently manage their revenue rather than creating ways of getting additional funds by increasing the tax burden.

Paine noticed that "we still find the greedy hand of government thrusting itself into every corner and crevice of industry, and grasping the spoil of the multitude. Invention is continually exercised, to furnish new pretenses for revenue and taxation. It watches prosperity as its prey, and permits none to escape without tribute." The results, he concludes, of excessive and unequal taxation, never fail to appear. "Whatever the apparent cause of any riots may be....it shows that something is wrong in the system of government." The Stamp Act and the Whiskey Rebellion are two good examples of reactions to unfair taxes.

Jefferson considered unnecessary officials as parasites on the public purse and took double delight in suppressing taxes and tax collectors. He boasted, "It may be the pleasure and pride of an American to ask, what farmer, what mechanic, what laborer ever sees a taxgatherer of the United States?" He set a remarkable example of responsible government, which few, if any, officials have chosen to follow.

The anti-federalists feared that the power to tax would transmit to posterity the "latent seeds of future tyranny", (as it certainly has, with the continuing rollover of the national debt from one generation to the next).

Samuel Osgood informed John Adams of the danger in giving permanent funds to Congress. Special interest groups, i.e., banks, which predominate in more than a major part of the United States, will finally establish an arbitrary government in the United States, he warned. With the establishment of the central bank and federally chartered banks, this is precisely what has happened.

An interesting point was made that since Congress would be collecting the taxes, their agents would represent national interests rather than those of the states. Therefore, one fear was that if Congress were empowered to grant pensions and salaries, and multiply their dependents, the government of America would become an aristocracy of special interests and favors.

Needless to say, the anti-federalists foresaw many problems which have come home to tyrannize us today.

The Constitution forbids a "capitation or other direct tax...unless in proportion to the census or enumeration hereinbefore directed to be taken" (Article I, Section 9). Thus a sales tax placed only on luxury items was considered fair because those that could afford to pay it would. But direct taxes, such as an income tax, would leave no choice; they would have to be paid. There is no limit (short of creating a rebellion) on which to tax incomes. If merchandise is too heavily taxed, sales slacken.

In No. 22 of *The Federalist*, Hamilton proposes that the rich may be extravagant, the poor can be frugal, and private oppressions may always be avoided by a judicious selection of objects proper for such sales taxes. Since the income tax is the most obnoxious and detrimental tax, this chapter will concentrate on its effects.

The Income Tax or Sixteenth Amendment was passed in 1913. It called for a tax of one percent on taxable amounts over $20,000. The highest rate was six percent on amounts over $500,000. In 1913, it was truly a tax-the-rich scheme. But one cannot help notice the rates today. Coupled with the Social Security Tax, another direct capitation tax, the poor pay out far more than the rich.

Paterson calls attention to the fallacy that the money obtained from the rich goes to the poor. When money is taken by a hold-up man, it goes to the thief. If it is taken by a philanthropic organization, it goes to the organization. If it is collected by the government, it goes to the politicians. Neither does increased taxation of the rich lower the rate of taxation on the poor. In fact, it causes an increase in all taxation, because it requires more and more money to support government's profitless expenditures such as buildings, staffs, etc. Such a tax reaches down inchmeal until it expropriates a portion, not merely of the last dollar of a poor man, but of the first dollar he can earn.[2]

Has any one ever heard a politician say he has enough money? That taxes could be lowered? Never! There is no end to the upkeep of big buildings, plush offices, large staffs, in addition to endless programs for the "public" welfare. It is only human nature to build, expand, be creative and productive, whether one is a contractor, farmer, or politician. But while all other producers earn their money voluntarily in the marketplace giving value for value, government expropriates its income by force.

Churchill summed it up succinctly when he observed that the crime against society is not profit, but loss: "Private industry runs at a profit and uses the profit to expand producing capacity. Government industry runs at a loss and taxes the substance of the people to pay for its inefficiencies...." Thus, government's taxation appetite is insatiable.

Taxation does not even give value for value. High taxes do not necessarily mean more services. In an extensive study by Dr. Colin D. Campbell, Professor of Economics at Dartmouth College, two similar fiscal systems were compared: New Hampshire, with no sales and income taxes, and Vermont, with both taxes. The years between 1940-1974 were studied; the report concluded: 1) "The adaptation of broad-based taxes in Vermont has contributed to the rise in ratio of taxes to personal income and to the rapid expansion of the major types of state and local government expenditures." 2) "There is little evidence that public services are better in Vermont than in New Hampshire despite the higher tax burden." 3) "The burden of state and local government debt has become much greater in Vermont than in New Hampshire." Thus, the experiment in big government is over and the verdict is in: IT FAILED!

The income tax is far more unjust to the poor and laboring groups, however. That a majority should be able to impose a discriminatory tax burden on a minority, is no less a form of tyranny than the rich thinking that taxing the poor, because there are so many more of them, will benefit the rich. This is a classical example of how to polarize the populace: rich *vs.* poor. Where different groups try to use the taxing system for personal advantage, the outcome must be social unrest and discontent.

A group of Pennsylvania Anti-Federalists in 1787 stated that giving Congress the power of direct taxation, however "oppressive in its nature and unequal in its operation, is certain as to its produce and simple in its collection; it cannot be evaded like the objects of imposts or excise, and will be paid, because all that a man has will he give for his head [capitation tax]. This tax is so congenial to the nature of despotism that it has ever been a favorite under such governments....

"The power of direct taxation will further apply to every individual, as Congress may tax land, cattle, trades, occupations, etc., to any amount, and every object of internal taxation is of that nature that, however oppressive, the people will have but this alternative—either to pay the tax or let their property be taken, for all resistance will be vain."[3]

Such was the fear of the power to tax. To repeat, Article I, Section 9 of the Constitution states: "No capitation or other direct tax shall be laid, *unless in proportion to the census or enumeration hereinbefore directed to be taken.*" (Emphasis added.) The income tax was declared unconstitutional in the late 1800s when it was first passed as a law. To circumvent this, an amendment was added to the Constitution to permit an income or "other direct tax." This opened the door to every possible tax on income: wages, commissions, services, corporate, dividend, capital gains, self-employment, unemployment, security transactions, personal property, royalties, inventories, tips, business sales, licenses, etc. Note how each form of income or property has been given a specific name, which just happens to correspond to a specific tax. The Income Tax Amendment also paved the way for state, city, and local income taxes.

The Income Tax Amendment, or Sixteenth Amendment, reads: "The Congress shall have the power to lay and collect taxes on incomes, from whatever source derived, without apportionment among the several States, and without regard to any census or enumeration." This is in direct opposition to the letter and spirit of the Constitution. In fact, Hamilton, in No. 36 of *The Federalist*, says, "Let it be recollected that the proportion of these taxes is not to be left to the discretion of the national legislature....An actual census or enumeration of the people must furnish the rule, a circumstance which effectually shuts the door to partiality or oppression," or so he thought.

Is there any doubt that the Sixteenth Amendment directly violates and contradicts the Constitution? It is similar to passing an amendment which denies each citizen his right to life, liberty, property and pursuit of happiness; in essence that is exactly what it is! This rank violation of justice is nothing less than tyranny. It can only yield slavery, not freedom. Indeed, Congressman Philip Crane from Illinois was quoted as saying that today "government at all levels is taking approximately 40% of personal income. Can we then insist that we are still free men or are not we in at least a stage of bondage where a majority of our lives are being spent according to the dictates of other people's consciences?" He warned that unless government growth and spending is checked, "by 1985 we're going to be flirting with 100% of our lives spent according to the dictates of other peoples' consciences." (Monex International Ltd., July-August, 1975 newsletter.)

After more than sixty years of existence, the income tax has so acquainted the public with its abuses, few see its insidious effects. It has been accepted as the normal, rather than the perverse. One example, in the *L.A. Times* of April 7, 1975, reports that the Internal Revenue Service has been using clandestine intelligence-gathering activities to spy on citizens. Another example of modern tyranny comes from sworn testimony before a Senate committee that the procedures, methods, and rules used by the I.R.S. are arbitrary, dictatorial, and unconstitutional, that the I.R.S. deliberately defrauds the citizens of their legal rights.

The record of the I.R.S. shows it illegally picks locks, cracks safes, steals records, tapes telephones, harasses, bullies, threatens, and imposes arbitrary and unjustifiable assessments on innocent and virtually helpless citizens. It seizes bank deposits, safe deposit box contents, wages, automobiles, homes, and anything else it can get its hands on. All this is done without leave of court, without due process of law, without court order, and without trial. Because its methods are so illegal, restricting them to legal means would render the I.R.S. powerless and put them out of business.[4]

The finest expose written on the income tax is Frank Chodorov's *The Income Tax, Root of All Evil.*[5] In its compact 133 pages, Chodorov covers all the evil aspects of the income tax; it is highly recommended to the reader. Here are presented some of the most insidious and tyrannical effects of the income tax.

In the beginning, "the worker was told that he was not paying an income tax when his pay envelope was opened and robbed; he was simply making a 'contribution' to 'insurance'." Of course, it is obvious today that the U.S. Treasury collects the tax and disperses it from the general fund, none is set aside for future obligations. Any private company who promised insurance and spent the premiums would be sued for fraud and put out of business. Furthermore, proportionately, the poor pay a higher percentage of Social Security Tax than those in a higher tax bracket.

Although the income tax appeals to those who seek an easy source of government funds, the politicians are the major beneficiaries of the income tax. It is the means by which politicians can increase their own incomes and importance. They can expand their power by promising gifts, grants, subsidies and the like. So political ambition plays a large role in retaining income taxation. The net result is that a large part of the populace is supported by unearned wealth, which is produced by their hard-working brethren.

A more obvious effect is that of income tax upon the right to property—the right to keep the fruits of one's labor and one's life. The government, in effect, is denying our right to property by claiming some part of our income. It allows us to keep some of it, because it recognizes our need, *not* our right; and whatever it grants us, is for the government to decide.

In addition, income and inheritance taxes imply the denial of private property. And since there is no limit to the amount of taxes demanded, the government can and often does confiscate everything one has earned or inherited. This places the government in the position of holding a prior lien on all the income, wealth, and property of its citizens. This negation of property rights is nothing less than socialism, where denial of private property is the first tenet. And the denial of the right to property is, in essence, the denial to the right to one's life, i.e., slavery. Furthermore, it should be remembered that if one citizen's rights are infringed, if one citizen's life is unsafe, then all citizens' rights and lives are unsafe from government encroachment and tyranny.

Since the Sixteenth Amendment stands as a direct contradiction to the right to our very existence, it would be well to repeat two very worthy observations at this time: "Every man is born with...a right before any other man, to inherit, with his brethren his father's goods," declared John Locke. And: "A people averse to the institution of private property is without the first element of freedom," warned Lord Acton.

Another destructive effect of the income tax is the denial that "all men are created equal." By taxing various groups at various rates a caste system is set up. Political favors are for sale to one group at the expense of another group. With "revenue sharing," witness states vying for federal government handouts, selling our liberties. The states, which were to be our first line of defense against tyranny, are now in the forefront, grabbing as much of the spoils as they can lay their hands on.

We have, in effect, an aristocracy that lives off the production of others—the bureaucracy is high up the social ladder. In fact, the two most affluent counties in the United States are Montgomery County, Maryland and Fairfax County, Virginia, both suburbs of Washington, D.C. Jefferson recognized the problem in 1824 in a letter to William Ludlow: "I think we have more machinery of government than is necessary, too many parasites living on the labour of the industrious."

In addition, the Sixteenth Amendment has corrupted the morals of the country. A farmer gets paid for not planting; a mother allows the government to give her child free school lunches; businessmen go hat-in-hand to Washington for protective tariffs; professors, on subsidies or grants, teach the benefits of central planning and big government; public education touts the income tax and the benefits of redistributing the wealth by the use of the progressive income tax. Today, where are individual rights respected and taught? Self-responsibility has been replaced by a paternal government; government handouts are no longer considered a degradation or, at best, a charity, but a "right." (These are the new "economic" rights.) Self-respect has been eroded away; and a people without self-respect have no use for freedom. Human dignity has suffered its greatest defeat. It forces taxpayers to lie and cheat in order to hold onto a portion of their earnings. The income tax has made criminals out of otherwise honest, hard-working citizens. All are corrupted by this devious Amendment.

The Internal Revenue Service, charged with enforcing the Sixteenth Amendment, has created a new police force, not to protect individual rights, but to violate them for the purpose of confiscating the individual's wealth, for the good of the state. This "end-justifies-the means" philosophy is anti-American and unjust; it is an excuse to run roughshod over the lives of others. The I.R.S. seeks to secure as much wealth for the government as possible, short of producing a revolt. Under the protection of law, it violates nearly every one of the Bill of Rights, abuses every shred of common decency, and sets itself up as lord and master of the people. As the I.R.S. is charged with the duty of enforcing an immoral law, it makes a mockery of our traditions of republican government, liberty, and justice. It deems a taxpayer guilty until proven innocent—a return to Napoleonic Law and absolutely tyrannical!

The income tax allows profits and capital accumulation to be siphoned off to the government, which hurts business. It holds back new competition while favoring older, well-established firms. Again it sets up a caste system, thwarting free enterprise, re-establishing mercantilism, where everyone must first get permission from the powers that be to start and remain in business; it is also known as socialism. Progressive taxation destroys capital formation, jobs, progress, and the country's high standard of living. In fact, Mill describes our form of progressive income taxation as "a mild form of robbery."[6]

As the citizen is sovereign only when he can retain and enjoy the fruits of his labor, taxes on income have produced a government far more powerful than George III ever exercised. Elections are merely a changing of the guard. Whoever is elected keeps the power already attained and, more often than not, tries to augment it. The end result is the liquidation of all individual rights and the creation of a regime of total government—totalitarianism.

We are already at the point where a taxpayer has fewer rights than an accused murderer:

	Accused Murderer	Taxpayer
Is innocent until proven guilty	Yes	No
Is informed of his constitutional rights	Yes	No
Need not give evidence against himself	Yes	No
Is entitled to trial by jury	Yes	No
Prosecutor may not also be the judge	Yes	No
May not be prosecuted on basis of illegally obtained evidence	Yes	No
May not be punished on testimony of secret informers who cannot be cross examined	Yes	No
May not be subjected to fines and punishments without due process of law	Yes	No

In sum, I.R.S. agent Thomas Mennitt best described the illegal nature of the tax collection policies: "I violate laws at all times, it's part of my duties." Former Congressman Wilbur Mills once called the I.R.S. a "House of Horrors."

Where does the blame for this injustice lie? With everyone, of course. The politicians' first concern is to be elected; his second is to be re-elected. For this, he is prepared to buy the votes he needs with favors made possible by income taxation; and whoever sells his vote also makes it possible. Such is an inherent weakness in popular government—democracy. The poor see something-for-nothing, little realizing they are the prey. Bankers and industrialists are also to blame. They line up for tariff protection and the like, along with veterans, retired people, unemployeds, farmers, educators, environmentalists, scientists, and the list goes on. Freedom and self-reliance are out of style. If anyone should suggest that this unjust form of paternalism be stopped and the income tax repealed, he would probably receive short shrift from the public. Who ever hears of honest work as the only way to get rich nowadays?

The kind of government we are acquiring is distinctly different from that promised and guaranteed by the Constitution. The change has been a peaceful revolution—the Revolution of 1913, as Chodorov calls it. Once the government was weak, unbothersome, subsisting on tariffs and a few excise taxes; the people were strong, self-reliant, independent. Today the government, living off the labor of the citizens, is strong, dictatorial; the people are weak, dependent and becoming poor.

The solution to this quagmire may seem too simple, but it is the only one that will work. The Sixteenth Amendment must be repealed and the control and responsibility of the American people returned to them individually for their own supervision.

We must be made to see the principle. No form of income, wealth, or property taxes is conducive to free people. The entire tax system is based on the voluntary cooperation of the victim. Only your sanction can continue the system. This system of bluff was corroborated by Senator Henry Bellman of Oklahoma: "In a recent conversation with an official at the Internal Revenue Service, I was amazed when he told me that, 'If the taxpayers of this country ever discovered that the Internal Revenue Service operates on ninety percent bluff, the entire system will collapse.' "[7]

To render ineffective the illegal coercive powers of the I.R.S., the citizens need only to understand their rights under the Constitution and have the courage to demand them.In the biggest betrayal in history; your own elected officials are selling you out and throwing you to the wolves; you are being sold into slavery by your own financing. The government certainly cannot be counted on to protect you. The only way to stop this process is to cut the government off at the purse-strings and show a little fighting spirit—that is the only language tyrants understand.

The actual results of this subversive Amendment could have been and were predicted. But everyone was too busy thinking about his share of the loot. Some spoke out against its adoption, but they were few and far between, as were the listeners. As early as January 26, 1894, Representative Robert Adams, for example, warned, "The imposition of the [income] tax will corrupt the people. It will bring in its train the spy and the informer. It will necessitate a swarm of officials with inquisitorial powers. It will be a step toward centralized [government].... It breaks another canon of taxation in that it is expensive in its collection and cannot be fairly imposed;...and, finally, it is contrary to the traditions and principles of republican government."

The income tax is truly the root of all evil.

And you, the victim, are sanctioning it.

To become a tax rebel at this time is one's patriotic duty. Once you are convinced that the Federal Reserve System and the Internal Revenue Service are ruining the nation and enslaving the people, you can do no less. Tax rebels are actuated by the highest principles of patriotism when they demand a return to Constitutional government. They are not opposed to the law; on the contrary, they are demanding that the law of the land be observed and enforced.[8] To ignore the situation is to condone the actions of tyrants. It is time to revere justice, to stand on principle, and to give not an inch!

Patriots, take hope: by a 2:1 majority millions of Californians have begun the "good fight." On June 6, 1978, Proposition 13 ("Jarvis-Gann") swept to victory, mandating a drastic cut in property taxes and providing rigorous safeguards against any compensatory rise in taxes. The tax rebellion is here now. We must seize this golden opportunity.

All over the nation there is a rebellion going on against oppressive and crippling taxation. The people are contemplating redress. Rebellion against taxes is an old American tradition—dating back to the founding of the republic and before.

We saved the best for last. There are over *three million* signatures on the "Yes on 23" petition. The full name of this petition is House Joint Resolution 23 or the Liberty Amendment to the Constitution. Once passed, it will *abolish the federal income tax* and eliminate government corporations that compete with private enterprise. Also, a proposal sponsored by Senators Mark Hatfield (R-Ore.) and James Abourezk (D-S.D.) and by Representatives Harold Sawyer and Guy Vander Jagt (both R-Mich.) would allow citizen initiative of laws on a national level. Under it only 2.5 million petition signatures would be needed to put an issue to a vote.

Furthermore, Liberty Lobby (300 Independence Ave. SE, Washington, D.C. 20003) has announced it will distribute "Yes on 23" petitions free to all interested patriots who write to them. (*Spotlight*, October 16, 1978, P. 24.)

Well, what are you waiting for?

NOTES ON TAXATION, CHAPTER XVI

1. Op. Cit., P. 96.
2. Op. Cit., Pp. 168-69.
3. Op. Cit., Pp. 183-84.
4. Marvin L. Cooley, *The Big Bluff—Tax Tyranny in the Guise of Law*, 525 E. Baseline Road, Mesa Arizona 85204, 1972, $5.
5. (Old Greenwich, Conn.: The Devin-Adair Co., 1974), P. 53.
6. Op. Cit., P. 308.
7. Cooley, *The Big Bluff.*
8. Martin A. Larson, *Tax Revolt: U.S.A! Why and How Thousands of Patriotic Americans Refuse to Pay the Income Tax*, Liberty Lobby, 300 Independence Avenue, S.E., Washington, D.C. 20003, 1973, $5.

XVII

Education

A general State education is a mere contrivance for moulding people to be exactly like one another: and the mould in which it casts them is that which pleases the predominant power in the government, whether this be a monarch, a priesthood, an aristocracy, or the majority of the existing generation; in proportion as it is efficient and successful, it establishes a despotism over the mind, leading by natural tendency to one over the body.

J.S. MILL

Of all the problems this country faces, the educational system is one of the most critical. Here again the culprit is government. The state and federal governments have taken nearly absolute control of the educational process, resulting in less education for more money. A deeper issue is, however, the state-oriented (socialist) curriculum which is being taught. Individual rights, freedom, justice, and free enterprise are all but gone from studies. Instead, big government, the "fairness" of redistributing other people's wealth, the benefits of government regulations, etc., are taught in every way, from kindergarten through university. Our children are not being taught how to think and act as free people. They are taught social virtues like conformity; they are taught how to get a job, how to get along with their peers, how to approach government for loans, etc. They do not know how to question, to judge, or to value. Blind followers cannot become self-sufficient, self-reliant, independent citizens. This is the result of government-run education. The solution is simple: separate government and education; education should be private and competitive.

Education has always been very dear to Americans. So important, in fact, that parents usually taught their children how to read and write at the earliest possible age. Franklin believed a man's life should be dedicated to being rational, disciplined, and ordered. Self-taught, Franklin proclaimed a reign of reason, knowledge, and wisdom; he praised mathematics. He announced, "Reading makes a full man; meditation a profound man; discourse a clear man."

Another remarkable Founding Father was Jefferson, whose I.Q. has been figured at 150, ranking him with Galileo, Michelangelo, and other geniuses. Jefferson's approach to the world was through his understanding of reality, rather than through his feelings. Someone said of Jefferson he could calculate an eclipse, survey an estate, tie an artery, plan an edifice, try a cause, break a horse, dance a minuet, and play a violin; he could also read Greek and Roman classics in the original. He hated indolence second only to tyranny. He studied fifteen hours every day while in college; and never stopped reading afterward, amassing the most extensive library in the colonies—totaling some 10,000 books.

Jefferson said of his youth: "I was bold in the pursuit of knowledge, never fearing to follow truth and reason to whatever results they led, and bearding every authority which stood in their way."

He was an ideologist, believing that correct theory, alike in politics and economics, is necessary to sound practice. His advice on studying was to keep one's attention fixed on the main objects of all science, the *freedom and happiness of man.* So that when the time came to bear their responsibility in government, young adults would keep always in view the sole object of all legitimate government.

Words were Jefferson's fortresses of thought; slovenly and inaccurate writing was no friend of truth or science. He wrote to the president of Harvard that his own generation had spent the majority of its time procuring the "precious blessing of liberty." Therefore, Harvard should spend its time showing that a nation will be great in both science and virtue in proportion to the degree that it is free.

Another example of an excellent education is that of Mill, whose father structured his comprehensive educational program. It began with Greek and arithmetic at the age of three. By the age of eight Mill had read six dialogues of Plato and considerable history. Before he was twelve he had studied Euclid, algebra, Greek and Latin poems, and some English poetry. At twelve he was introduced to Aristotle's logic. His thirteenth year, the last one under his father's direction, was devoted to political economy. By fourteen he was equipped with a thorough university education.

Nowadays, the educational system is not educating people for a free society, as Mill's father did; instead youth are being trained to be "used." They are not taught how to think but how to fit into a niche in society, which they expect somebody to provide.

Hayek reminds us that "the more highly one rates the power that education can have over men's minds, the more convinced one should be of the danger of placing this power in the hands of any single authority."[1] No superior must be allowed to enforce one set of views of what is right or good, for liberty shows its ultimate value when human development is in its richest diversity.

It is the socialists who try to collect children from the tenderest age to ensure the production of "good socialist followers." It is significant that the nationalization of thought (through government-supported education) has proceeded hand-in-glove with government directed industry, economics, politics, and morality, undermining everywhere our sense of truth and justice.

On a lighter note, Mencken wrote an article for the Baltimore *Evening Sun* on October 8, 1928, in which he talked about school days. In general, he said, school days are full of tortures. They "are full of...brutal violations of common sense and common decency. It doesn't take a reasonably bright boy long to discover that most of what is rammed into him is nonsense....His first teachers he views simply as disagreeable policemen. His later ones he usually sets down quite accurately as asses."[2]

Regarding corporal punishment, Mencken said the school he attended resorted to rattanning when needed. Its effects, he was convinced, were excellent. It preserved the self-respect of the teachers, and tended to earn the boys' respect. Given command, they actually exercised it. He never heard of a complaint from a student for having been used cruelly or unjustly.

Mencken concludes that in "the whole realm of human learning there is no faculty more fantastically incompetent than that of pedagogy....The new pedagogy has got so complicated that it often forgets the pupil altogether....It is...converting the children into laboratory animals. I believe that the old sing-song system, with an occasional fanning of the posterior, was better. At all events, it was simpler. One could grasp it without graphs."[3]

In his *The Memoirs of A Superfluous Man*, Nock describes the private education he received in his youth. His father had chosen the school; it was one of the last ones with "the grand old fortifying classical curriculum." Nock learned to appreciate it more as time went by when he saw what passed for education in the public schools, where he taught college for two years.

The old system was based on work, self-responsibility, and justice. In this way, the students developed respect for their instructors and a desire to learn the material presented. Nock says, "The authorities had nothing to do with us in a social way; our only contact with them was in business hours and for business purposes. They were men of vast learning, great dignity, always punctiliously polite, but with no affectation of cordiality. For our part, we put up no pretense of fondness for them, but our respect, pride, admiration of them, knew no bounds. We would have fought for them like Stonewall Jackson's soldiers, at the drop of a hat. Their character impressed us even more than their learning, great as that was; and their aloofness just suited us, because it was so completely in character. If they had once tried to make themselves informal, chummy, big-brotherly—in a word, vulgar—we would have resented it with contempt. No student was ever spoken to, or spoken of, as Jim or Bill, Smith or Jones, but always as Mr. Smith or Mr. Jones. Our preceptors were gentlemen as well as scholars."

Children need to look up to their elders and teachers. They actually want to learn and understand, and not have their emotions and whims catered to. They are trying to find heroes and "good guys." This is a normal part of growing up. The classical school instructors realized this. They showed respect for each student individually and received it in return. In an environment of respect and knowledge a lot of learning can take place, and it did.

Nock continues, "There was not a grain of sentimentalism in the institution; on the other hand, the place was permeated by a profound sense of justice. The most important extra-curricular lesson we learned—and we learned it properly—was summed up in Chief Justice Jay's dictum that 'justice is always the same, whether it be due from one man to a million, or from a million to one man.' We learned this, not by precept, but by example, which is the best way to learn such lessons. In all circumstances we were treated justly, never coddled or pampered, but never overborne or sat upon. Each day's work was a full day's work.... We were made to understand that the burden of education was on us and no one else, least of all our instructors; they were not there to help us carry it or to praise our efforts, but to see that we shouldered it in proper style and got on with it."

If Nock and his classmates were taught the full value of justice, the highest social virtue, what a magnificent lesson. It is the direct opposite of the lessons taught today. No wonder they were prepared for life and contemporary children are not.

Nock then describes the curriculum they received. "Our academic course was fixed and unchangeable as the everlasting hills....Elective courses, majors and minors...were unknown to us; we had never heard of them." Nor did they miss them; it is the students of the last 40 to 50 years who are the real losers. Here is what Nock received for an education: "Readings and expositions of Greek and Roman literature [in the original of course]; mathematics up to the differential calculus; logic; metaphysics; a little work on the sources and history of the English language; these made up the lot. If you were good at it, you were given a bachelor's degree at the end of four years, and you were then expected to get out promptly and not come back. The incursions of alumni were most distasteful to the authorities, and were firmly disallowed. If, on the other hand, you were not good enough to stand the appointed strain, it was presumably a matter of God's will, and nothing could be done about it."

It is fascinating to learn the benefits of studying ancient history. As Nock explains, the literatures of Greece and Rome cover nearly twenty-five hundred years in poetry, drama, law, agriculture, philosophy, architecture, natural history, philology, rhetoric, astronomy, logic, politics, botany, zoology, medicine, geography, theology—everything in the range of human knowledge or speculation. "Hence the mind which has attentively canvassed this record is much more than a disciplined mind, it is an experienced mind." Santana said those who are ignorant of history are doomed to repeat it. Santana himself could not have designed a better course of learning.

Another benefit from this type of education is that it leaves the mind uncluttered by a lot of concrete facts; it allows the mind to think in abstract form, and more importantly, it allows new ideas and circumstances "free entrance to an unpreoccupied mind." As Plato said of an educated man, he should be able and always willing, to "see things as they are."

Nock explains that the type of education he received is called "formative knowledge." The other type, which is taught in public schools today exclusively, is "instrumental knowledge." His preceptors "painstakingly kept clear the difference" between the two. "They had the theory that a young man who had gone through their mill could turn his hand to anything in the whole range of intellectual or manual pursuits, and do it to better advantage in the long-run than one who had not."[4]

It is no wonder that the majority of great industrialists came from this school of thinking. Today there are only followers and complainers, no more thinkers. Cicero proclaimed the truth in saying those who have no knowledge of history must forever remain children. Nowadays, the best description of the product of our schools is "immaturity."

Next Nock delves into the revolution in education, which drastically purged and thoroughly guillotined the classical curriculum, to substitute in its place the "elective system." Under the democratic belief that all people are teachable, gifts, grants, subsidies, and endowments poured into schools, colleges and universities. The result has been a system that resembles "a huge bargain-counter or a modern drug-store."

The worst result has been a complete obliteration of the line separating education from training, and formative knowledge from instrumental knowledge. This "was done deliberately to meet the popular perversions of equality and democracy." The new system calls "training" education. It gives courses in business, bricklaying, and basket-weaving and calls them an education. It puts on the same show of pomp and circumstance, including academic degrees and cap and gowns. The greatest lessons learned are that agreeing with the opinions of others produces power and that small minds are equal to great minds.

The greatest fraud perpetrated is that graduates actually believe they are educated and thinking citizens. They think they are articulate when they are not. Mediocrity and submediocrity run rampant, to the detriment of both intelligence and taste. The system has succeeded only in making them more gullible and easily led.

There is a vast difference between education and training. Education—a process leading to intelligence and wisdom, employing formative knowledge—produces something in the way of an Emerson, says Nock. Whereas training—a process leading to sagacity and cleverness, employing instrumental knowledge—produces something in the way of an Edison. Of course, it must be "properly applied to suitable material" in both cases.

In conclusion, Nock says, "Our system was founded in all good faith that universal elementary education would make a citizenry more intelligent; whereas most obviously it has done nothing of the kind." If Jefferson, one of the promoters of public, mass education, could return to the republic and see what his pet project had come to—"a levelling agency, prescribing uniform modes of thought, belief, conduct, social deportment, diet, recreation, hygiene," Nock says, "I believe he would regard the entire exhibit with unstinted disgust and contempt."[5]

Paterson also takes to task today's progressive educational system in America. She writes that the old-fashioned education gave the teacher power to discipline, imparted positive facts and principles, discouraged immature self-expression, sought to strengthen character by self-control of the social impulse, and attached responsibility to any child disobedient of rules. Furthermore, it taught children to think by use of formal logic on impersonal examples, while current issues were kept out of the classroom.

In contrast, the progressive system today forbids positive punishment and encourages immature self-expression in youngsters and social-mindedness in older pupils. It tries to teach by experiment, discussion, and debate on current topics, omitting principles.

The old system aimed at cultivating individual ability and personal character—the creation of an independent, thinking, forceful being. The new system creates blind followers who lack any sense of morals or justice. Neither evidence nor logic penetrate the fog within their minds.

The old system taught reading by the phonetic alphabet, the great value of which is that the tools for reading are put into the pupil's possession very quickly. Once the twenty-six letters of the alphabet are learned along with the principle of their combination, as indicated by sounds, the student knows how to read. The phonetic alphabet is one of the greatest labor-saving devices man ever invented, says Paterson.

On the other hand, the progressive system teaches by memorizing countless words, never quite teaching one *how* to read. It wastes a great deal of time, stunts reading potential, and handicaps the process of abstract thought severely.

Another flaw of the new system is its procedure for grading. The old way of grading by the 60,70,80,90 percentile was objective. The new way of grading "on a curve" is horribly unfair to students. One can never know if one has learned the material or not; the acquisition of knowledge becomes relative. It hurts the negligent child, who thinks he is getting away with something and finds out much too late he got away with no education. It deprives the conscientious child of an earned benefit or reward. In addition, the teacher is isolated from finding out whether he taught the material adequately. It is a totally unjust method of grading.

"So in every way," says Paterson, "the natural outlet of energy in human beings which in childhood is properly directed toward the development of intelligence and character, is choked down and subverted: the purpose of study is not to learn things which are true in themselves nor to develop independence through such knowledge, but to please and conform to arbitrary authority."[6]

In contrast, Paterson cites the benefits of private schools, which vary in curriculum, must compete for students, are directly tied to payment of private funds, have no inducement to teach the "supremacy of the state" as a compulsory philosophy, and leave the parents in full control of their children's education.

The standard of education in America was much higher a hundred and fifty years ago than it is now, she asserts. Primer education was taught at home; most children entered school knowing how to read, write and perform simple arithmetic. Then if further education was desired parents could send their children to a choice of schools with various courses and various fees.

Would some children remain illiterate? They might, as some do now, as they did in the past. But at least they used to know they were illiterate. Today graduates of high schools, colleges, and universities are not aware of the fact. For example, as valedictorian of his class and a straight "A" student, an 18-year-old graduate of a Washington, D.C. inner-city high school figured to have no trouble qualifying for the college of his choice. But George Washington University turned down his application for admission when his College Board exams were only about half of what the school expected and when he did poorly on a special battery of tests administered by the university. This is an indictment of the permissive concepts of our educational system that "too often hoodwinks students." "My feeling about a kid like this, " said the dean of admissions at Gēorge Washington, "is that he's been conned. He thinks he's a real scholar. His parents think he's a real scholar. He's been deluded into thinking he's gotten an education." (*Wall Street Journal,* August, 26, 1976.)

Paterson concludes that there is no greater example of arbitrary power than seizing children from their parents, teaching them the government's dogma, and expropriating from the parents the funds to pay for the procedure. Two questions should be put to an indignant teacher who argues otherwise: "Do you think nobody would *willingly* entrust his children to you or pay you for teaching them? Why do you have to exact your fees and collect your pupils by compulsion?

The current educational system is triply coercive: compulsory attendance, compulsory curriculum, and compulsory financing (taxation). In short, "A tax-supported, compulsory educational system is the complete model of the totalitarian state," closes Paterson.[7]

Noah Webster in 1785 hit the nail on the head when he declared that ignorance cramps the powers of the mind at the same time that it blinds men to all their natural rights. Schools today are doing more evil than good. They teach nothing of true values, not even our political rights. Jefferson reaffirmed that "if a nation expects to be ignorant and free, in a state of civilization, it expects what never was and never will be." As we are becoming a nation of illiterates, so are we becoming a nation of slaves.

Mitchell Jones, editor of *The New Individualist,* has studied the effects of public versus private education on students. The evils he found are: 1) The basic system of learning emphasized is not comprehension or critical thinking, but rote memorization. 2) This doing of only minimum work to get by becomes a habit carried into adulthood resulting in lack of persistence and direction. 3) It is incomprehensible to modern man that any one would spend a lifetime on continuous intellectual growth, which was popular when ideas were respected. 4) Private schools accredited by government teach the same currriculum as public schools—government regulations have leveled down both. Private schools, however, are subject to a "negative feedback" from unhappy parents, which makes them inherently more responsive to consumer demands.

Jones sees public education as "a twelve-year, non-stop, frontal assault on the mind. It is a tribute to luck and the resilience of the human organism that anyone emerges from the system with any interest in ideas."[8]

Here are some statistics from *Moneysworth* (September 13, 1976) on the state of our educational system today: "During the 1965-66 school year, U.S. public schools spent $26.3 billion. Ten years later, that figure had risen to $66.8 billion, a 250% increase during a period that saw the overall cost of living rise by 71%....National tests indicate that the quality of education has been steadily deteriorating in such basic areas as reading, writing and arithmetic. Between 1962 and 1975, Scholastic Aptitude Test scores for the average high school senior declined 30 points in math and 44 points in verbal ability.... The only thing that seems to be on the rise in public schools are teacher salaries. The national average teacher salary has almost doubled in the past 10 years....These figures are deceptively low. The public must bear the cost of supplementary salaries, fringe benefits, retirement and leave benefits as well. When these are figured in, the New York City teacher, for example, has an income of approximately $30,288."

Regarding their power-lust, "the National Education Associaton (NEA) and the American Federation of Teachers claim 2.1 million members. Together, they represent a bargaining power in this country exceeded in number of members only by the Teamsters." And NEA president John Ryor has listed the No. 1 goal of his union as "becoming the foremost political power in the nation," not even mentioning the plummeting level of education.

Comments Dr. Kenneth Clark, a noted psychologist at the City University of New York, "If we ran any other institution as inefficiently as we run our schools, we'd all be in receivership by now."

The Libertarian Review, a monthly newsletter edited by Murray N. Rothbard, ran an essay by Auberon Herbert (1838-1906) in its September, 1976 issue. It was entitled: "Education by Bribes and Coercion." Herbert wrote of the British educational system of the late nineteenth century. His observations and remarks are extremely relevant to the United States today.

Herbert begins with the keen observation that whatever the state touches, it destroys. Since the state has laid its grasp on education, it has produced a curse rather than a blessing—an instrument of torture instead of a means to happiness and strength.

Parents have been ousted from control as government has assumed possession of a system that presses the whole nation into the same mold.

Herbert warns, "Some day you will see that there is no man so truly disinherited, as the man who once takes a State-bribe."

Then he proceeds to examine the system. First, it dreads competition and endeavors to exclude all rivals; second, it is built on those two most evil foundation-stones, coercion and state money. Third, it deserves hatred instead of gratitude because you cannot place hundreds of thousands of persons under the same system without repressing the differences that exist and ought to exist among them. In destroying these differences, all hope of progress is destroyed. Fourth, the system has become stupid, brutal, coercive, arrogant, and extravagant; its methods have made it rigid, mechanical, and oppressive. Fifth, it produces an unthinking nation. And lastly, it teaches the people the evil lesson of forcing one group to support the wants of another group. It degrades and corrupts everybody.

Since we have no right to persecute each other, he goes on to show how and why this system can be changed. The first thing is to return control of the children to their parents by rejecting all state funds, grants, and gifts. Then the people, "not made stupid by systems and codes, nor enervated by State-payments, could fulfill with their own hands and brains their necessities of life."

He appeals to the people to take a higher view of this question than they have ever yet taken. They should assume the responsibility of seeing that their children are adequately educated, not handed blindly over to state machinery.

Herbert advises the people to organize for liberty: Destroy compulsion in every form and under every disguise. Give to no man the power of carrying out his own ideas at the expense and compulsion of his neighbor. Allow to all the freedoms of choice and action, and to none the degradation of using his neighbor, or being himself used, against his convictions. And, finally, have confidence in moral force as opposed to all state-directed coercion. Re-discover the joy of seeing a job well done and of doing it without State aid.[9]

In 1970, Rand wrote an expose of the progressive educational system in a five-part series entitled: "The Comprachicos."[10] It explains the motives behind and results of the "modern" educational system in the United States.

The Comprachicos, explains Rand, were a hideous nomadic association, famous in the seventeenth century as buyers and sellers of children. They turned children into monsters via reverse orthopedics. They got hold of children early and through skill and surgery deformed the faces, bodies, and minds of their patients.

In Rand's translation of Victor Hugo's *The Man Who Laughs,* she says that the comprachicos did not merely remove a child's face, they removed as much of his memory as they could. The child was not aware of the mutilation he had suffered, since this horrible surgery left traces on his face, not in his mind.

The twentieth-century educator, claims Rand, is practicing the same skill, only with a different twist. Today we are still witnessing the production of helpless, twisted monsters whose normal development has been stunted. The children are not bought, but delivered up to the educators.

"In the past, this horrible surgery left traces on a child's face, not in his mind. Today, it leaves traces in the mind, not on his face. In both cases, the child is not aware of the mutilation he has suffered."

Today's educators put mental retardation where nature put a normal brain. She says nothing can be more ingenious than to make a person unconscious for life by means of one's own brain. This ingenuity is practiced by most modern educators, "the comprachicos of the mind."

They place a child into a "progressive" nursery school to adjust him to society. Their primary goal is "social adjustment" and conformity to the group. "At the age of five-and-a-half," says Rand, "he is ready to be released into the world: an impotent creature, unable to think, unable to face or deal with reality, a creature who combines brashness and fear, who can recite its memorized lessons, but cannot understand them—a creature deprived of its means of survival...." The monster is now made.

The next step is to "stunt, stifle and destroy the students' capacity to develop the use of abstractions—to think in principle. John Dewey, the father of modern education and the progressive nursery school, opposed the teaching of abstractions in favor of concrete, practical projects, which would develop the student's "social spirit or social mind." His aim was to produce not individualists, but conformists—easily manipulated robots.

The process of thinking—forming, integrating and using concepts—is not automatic, but volitional; it has to be learned. Man's entire future well-being and happiness depend on how well or how badly he learns to think. Adults can help the development of a child's reasoning faculty by providing an environment that is stable, consistent, and intelligible, which rewards the child's efforts to understand. Or they can harm it in an environment where reality is incomprehensible, unanswered, and unpredictable.

The method in use nowadays is that of rote memorization. The "Look-See" method of reading—of memorizing each word—strains the mind and yields the "reading neurosis" prevalent in today's culture. This inability to read did not exist prior to the "Look-See" method when phonetics were taught. The ultimate result is the college freshman who is unable to read, write, spell, and speak coherently—all caused by the inability to organize his thoughts, if he has any.

The system succeeds in producing full-fledged socialists, reciting dogma, bromides, and catch-phrases of which they have not the slightest understanding. This socialist mentality forms adults who become violators of individual rights. They have been taught to disrespect their peers' minds and property, as all are "equal" (in ability, thinking, etc.) *or should be*! The logical step is to persecute anyone smarter, healthier, wealthier, or just different from the rest of the group, society, or mob.

This happens logically, because the educational system has taught students, who are now adults, to react, not act; to respond, not initiate; to pursue pleasure, not purpose. The theme is clear—attack the intellect; hate reason, proclaim emotions. (How utterly opposite from Jefferson's education.) The progressive educator strives not to enlighten, but to cripple his students.

The next step is college, where students hear it explicitly declared "that it is wrong, naive or futile to seek knowledge." There are no absolutes; everything is relative. If the process was not completed before college entrance, it is now.

The majority of students, deprived of the ability to reason, become pliable clay, ready to be shaped into any form or used for any purpose by anyone who wants to bother. And there is never a shortage of "manipulators" always seeking power over others, whether they be dictators, politicians, educators, psychologists, neurotic individuals, or religious fanatics.

"Power-lust requires guinea pigs," explains Rand, "to develop the techniques of inculcating obedience—and cannon fodder that will obey the orders. College students fill both roles." Now they need a master, a leader. Without one, they turn to drugs to escape their own anxieties, mindlessness, and fear. The phenomenon of nearly an entire generation resorting to drugs is proof of the failure of the progressive system.

Rand argues that since it is ideas that have produced this national disaster, it is ideas which must be used to change it. The anti-rational philosophy of socialism must be changed to the rational philosophy of individual rights, free enterprise, and freedom—the values of reason, purpose, and self-esteem. Nothing less will work.

Rand closes her essay with a quote from her book *Atlas Shrugged*, regarding one of the guiltiest groups, the parents:

"He thought of all the living species that train their young in the art of survival, the cats who teach kittens to hunt, the birds who spend such strident effort on teaching their fledgings to fly–yet man, whose tool of survival is the mind, does not merely fail to teach a child to think, but devotes the child's education to the purpose of destroying his brain, of convincing him that thought is futile and evil, before he has started to think....

"Men would shudder, he thought, if they saw a mother bird plucking the feathers from the wings of her young, then pushing him out of the nest to struggle for survival—yet *that* was what they did to their children."

Public education is a scourge. It must be wrested from government control and set up on a local basis. Eventually it should be turned over to free enterprise, where a real education can be obtained at a reasonable price. The Department of Health, Education and Welfare ought to be abolished immediately; it is an insult to all liberty-loving citizens. Let us fight to regain our rights, our property and our children!

In conclusion, here is the opinion of Bertrand Russell on state education given in 1955: "State education, in the countries which adopt [socialist] principles, produces, so far as it is successful, a herd of ignorant fanatics, ready at the word of command to engage in war or persecution as may be required of them. So great is this evil that the world would be a better place (at any rate, in my opinion) if State education had never been inaugurated."

NOTES ON EDUCATION, CHAPTER XVII

1. *Constitution of Liberty*, P. 380.
2. *Vintage Mencken*, Pp. 182-3.
3. IBID., Pp. 184-5.
4. Chicago: Henry Regnery Co., A Gateway Edition, 1969, Pp. 76-81.
5. IBID., Pp. 261 and 264-65.
6. Op. Cit., P. 268.
7. IBID., Pp. 272 and 274.
8. Aegis, P.O. Box 12963, Austin, Texas 78711, December, 1975, P. 2.
9. Box 341, Madison Square Station, New York, New York, 10010, Pp. 1-4.
10. *The Objectivist*, 201 East 34th St., New York, New York 10016, August-December, 1970.

XVIII
Guns

Could the peaceable principle of the Quakers be universally established, arms and the art of war would be wholly extirpated. But we live not in a world of angels. The reign of Satan is not ended; neither are we to expect to be defended by miracles.... I am thus far a Quaker, that I would gladly agree with all the world to lay aside the use of arms, and settle matters by negotiation; but unless the whole will, the matter ends, and I take up my musket and thank heaven he has put it in my power.

THOMAS PAINE

On March 5, 1770 there occurred a skirmish between British soldiers and Boston colonists, leaving five Bostonians dead. The incident swiftly became known as the "Boston Massacre."

Within minutes of the first shots the streets rang with the cry: "To arms! To arms! Turn out with your guns!" Nearly five hundred people assembled.

The following day Sam Adams issued an ultimatum to Governor Hutchinson's office. Unless there was total evacuation of British soldiers, the troops would be destroyed. Fifteen thousand armed citizens, thundered Adams, were ready and eager to march into Boston to eliminate the hated soldiers. Hutchinson was advised to surrender, and warned that all New England would soon rise in arms against the British troops. Before night fell, Hutchinson capitulated, and promised a speedy and complete evacuation of the troops.

What could Sam Adams have cried if arms had been outlawed? If not, "To arms! To arms! Turn out with your guns!" what could the battle cry have been, if any? Without arms, where could the colonists turn for support in their fight for freedom against tyranny and oppression?

Fortunately Sam Adams' threats were not idle ones. Forty thousand New Englanders were ready to march for the liberation of Boston. In fact, armed men had already begun arriving in Boston and had to be stopped by Bostonians announcing that the crisis was over for now.

The American Revolution was a struggle to regain and secure the individual rights that the colonists *had before* Britain started usurping them. From the beginning, the moral was clear—that *only* an *armed* people's militia could be relied upon to deal successfully with an enemy. From that time on militia groups were set up all over the colony. "Innocence is no longer safe," declared Adams in the *Boston Gazette:* "we are now obliged to appeal to God, and to our ARMS for defense."[1]

Although there was a lull after the Boston Massacre in 1770 until 1773, things began to heat up again by 1774. The Boston Tea Party, the Coercive Acts, the Quebec Act, they all had the same effect–to make more and more colonists realize the tyranny of the British crown and that a fight for freedom was inevitable.

Sam and John Adams both knew it would come down to a fight. "I expect no redress but...increased resentment and double vengeance," predicted John Adams. "We must fight."[2]

Massachusetts readied for war. The Committee of Safety proceeded to organize an armed militia, aiming to raise a potential army of twelve thousand men. The militia trained hard. Soon all the militia were directed to train according to Colonel Timothy Pickering's new book *Easy Plan of Discipline for a Militia* (1775). Pickering simplified the ritualistic rules of British army drill and emphasized the American character—the woodsman's habit of individual markmanship.

Pickering blended American political theory with military tactics. He "stressed that the American soldier was an individualist, a freeman, a property owner, in contrast to professional European soldiers trained as obedient 'machines.' " Pickering wrote that "men must see the reason and the use of any action or movement. 'Tis the boast [of European commanders] that their men are mere machines.... God forbid that my countrymen should be thus degraded...."[3]

In 1775 Massachusetts increased her defense measures. She authorized the militia to collect military stores rapidly. The people were exhorted to voluntarily support the cause of liberty: "Resistance to tyranny becomes the Christian and social duty of each individual. Fleets, troops, and every implement of war are sent into the province, to wrest from you that freedom which it is your duty, even at the risk of your lives, to hand inviolate to posterity. Continue steadfast, and...defend those rights which heaven gave, and no man ought to take from us."[4]

In March, 1775 the Virginia House of Burgesses met. Patrick Henry made his famous call to arms speech. He asked the assembly, who were unwilling to commit themselves to fight, when would they be strong enough to fight? "Will it be the next week, or the next year? Will it be when we are totally disarmed [by the British], and when the British guard be stationed in every house?... Three millions of people, armed in the holy cause of liberty, and in such a country as that which we possess, are invincible by any force which our enemy can send against us....Gentlemen may cry, Peace, Peace—but there is no peace. The war is actually begun! The next gale that sweeps from the north will bring to our ears the clash of resounding arms! Our brethren are already in the field [in Massachusetts]! Why stand we here idle? What is it that gentlemen wish? What would they have? Is life so dear, or peace so sweet, as to be purchased at the price of chains and slavery? Forbid it almighty God! I know not what course others may take; but as for me, give me liberty or give me death!"

Virginia fell into line and formed militia companies.

Could Henry have called the assembly to arms if arms had been outlawed? How could he have enlisted the aid of Virginians to support Massachusetts? With what weapons could the "holy cause of liberty" have been *fought* and *won?*

The British were unaware of the colonists intentions. In Parliament, the Earl of Sandwich, first lord of the Admiralty, contemptuously asked: "Suppose the colonies do abound in men, what does that signify? They are raw, undisciplined, cowardly men. I wish instead of...fifty thousand of these brave fellows, they would produce in the field at least two hundred thousand; the more the better; the easier would be the conquest...the very sound of a cannon would carry them off...as fast as their feet could carry them."

That was in April, 1775. Accordingly, secret orders were sent to General Gage to put down the colonists' "rebellion." But the colonists were not to be put down. Days later on April 19, 1775, the war began at Lexington and Concord.

The British march back to Boston from Concord was to become one of the most famous in the annals of America. The embattled and neighboring farmers and militiamen created a nightmare of destruction for the buoyant British. Knowing their home terrain intimately, these "raw, undisciplined, cowardly" individualistic Americans subjected the proud British troops to a continuous withering and overpowering fire from behind trees, walls and houses.

The American cause had a noble beginning. The British initiated the aggression and massacre with their arrogant troops. Then the angry and armed people of Massachusetts routed the enemy. The significance of Lexington and Concord touched off the general armed conflict proudly named the American Revolution.

For the fiftieth anniversary of the occasion, Emerson penned these immortal lines:

> By the rude bridge that arched the flood
> Their flag to April's breeze unfurled,
> Here once the embattled farmers stood
> And fired the shot heard round the world.

If the colonists had submitted to British tyranny piece by piece, law by law, no doubt by the time they decided to fight back it would have been too late. There would have been no rifle to fire the shot heard round the world. The time to fight tyranny is in the beginning, when the people still have their constitutional *rights, and arms* to protect and defend those rights. An unarmed populace is a ruled populace. *Only armed citizens are free* and can retain their freedom, by force, if necessary.

Jefferson once said, "The tree of liberty must be refreshed from time to time, with the blood of patriots and tyrants. It is its natural manure." Governments must be made to remember who holds the ultimate power—the people. The people must make a show of arms once in a while to put government, which has a tendency to forget who is boss, back in its place. It is all good and healthy for the country. Only an armed people hold the power to keep their government in check. Once unarmed, they are doomed.

The essence of current gun control legislation is people control. Either citizens rule their government or the government rules its citizens. It is either/or. And the balance of power falls to the most armed side.

In a related matter, the colonists understood the evils of a standing army. They violently opposed standing armies, believing that free people can defend themselves better than those dependent on a national armed force (which could be used against them). Therefore, every man owned a gun and knew how to use it, because he was the defensive force against enemy attack. A gun-controlled populace would have no choice but to submit to a national army, not to mention a foreign invasion.

In 1798 the United States Army was increased from 3,500 to 12,000 men. A hue and cry went up from all the colonies, which were deathly afraid of standing armies.

The following resolutions of Dinwiddie County, Virginia, appeared in the *Philadelphia Aurora* on December 6, 1798:

> *Resolved*, as the opinion of this meeting, that a militia, composed of the body of the people, is the proper, natural, and safe defense of a free state, and that regular armies, except in case of an invasion, are not only highly detrimental to the public welfare but dangerous to liberty.
>
> *Detrimental to the public welfare;* because industrious men are heavily taxed to support those who do nothing; because indolence among the poor is publicly encouraged; the army being an asylum for all who do not choose to labor; because the young men who form the mass of an army, instead of being a drawback on the productive labor of the community might be more beneficially employed in supporting, by their industry, themselves and their families and paying their proportions of the public debt; because the same object, immediate defense against a sudden invasion, might be attained infinitely cheaper by putting arms into the hands of every man capable of bearing them; and because the spirit which leads to war, the cause and the disgrace of humanity, is greatly augmented by standing armies, to whose leaders it opens a prospect of greater wealth and higher military honors; and,
>
> *Dangerous to liberty;* because, when numerous, they have tyrannized, as the experience of all ages has proved, both over the people and the government; and when limited, have always been subservient to the views of the Executive Department, from which they derive their honors and emoluments; because these honors and emoluments furnish an ample fund, by means of which the executive is enabled to reward its partisans and increase the number of its adherents; because a people, accustomed to look for protection from external violence to a standing army, become abject, debased, and gradually enslaved; but knowing themselves to be the only defenders of their country, soon acquire that discipline and courage which insure safety, not only from foreign enemies but domestic tyrants; and because military establishments are in their nature progressive, the vast expense attending them, producing discontent

> and disturbances, and these furnishing a pretext for providing a force still more formidable; thus finally occasioning the oppression, the ruin, the *slavery* of the people."[5]

Noah Webster points out that a standing army is the instrument of tyranny and ought to be forever banished from free governments. Not only do we have and support a vast standing army today; it stands, at our expense, on foreign soil. If gun control legislation passes and succeeds in disarming American citizens, this vast army may come home to roost. There is an alternative, however.

Jefferson agreed that "Every national citizen must wish to see an effective instrument of coercion, and should fear to see it on any other element but the water. A naval force can never endanger our liberties, nor occasion bloodshed; a land force would do both."[6]

The brilliant Alden Wells has written a thought-provoking booklet entitled: *The New Monroe Doctrine, Role of the Navy*, which explains how to replace the Army and Air Force with a Navy and Marine Corps. The new system would be far more efficient, far less expensive, a greater deterrent to foreign aggression, and conducive to world peace. George Washington gave us the best advice on foreign policy: 1) "No entangling alliances;" 2) "No standing army;" 3) "A well equipped and maintained Navy." Wells begins:

> From Wilson on we have ignored the first two and are now beginning to ignore the third.
>
> Despite Washington's clear advice, despite our impregnable position on the Western Hemisphere...we stumbled into one European war after another, and then Asian wars.
>
> We have neglected the most important element of our foreign policy, the sovereignty of the seas.
>
> There is a date line down the middle of the Pacific running from pole to pole. A similar one is easily drawn down the Atlantic. Let the United States unilaterally declare that Western Hemisphere territorial waters extend to those two lines. No claim is made beyond them.
>
> We should give up all our foreign bases, fleets, financial aid, and C.I.A. in order to concentrate our Naval strength in the Western Hemisphere and the oceans surrounding them.
>
> The Monroe Doctrine announced unilaterally that the United States would not tolerate attempts by the old world to increase its territory in the new world. The New Monroe Doctrine declares that sovereignty of the states

> of the Western Hemisphere begins half-way across the Atlantic and Pacific.
>
> Admiral Rickover, against many obstacles, has built a nuclear powered submarine fleet that can fire ICBM's. Placing such missiles on land is a waste of money because they are easily spotted and other ICBM's permanently aimed to destroy them. The submarine fleet should be our deterrent.
>
> With a proper foreign policy we could properly equip the Navy, including its air arm and the marines, but dispense with the army and air force....If the savings are used to reduce debt and taxes, the prospect for an enduring peace and prosperity will return for the first time this century."[6]

How simple it is when things are done rationally. It is interesting to note that the free Republic of Switzerland has no standing army. Instead, every able-bodied man between the ages of 18 and 45 owns a rifle and is trained to use it. It is an old Swiss tradition that only an armed man can have political rights; Switzerland also has one of the lowest crime rates. A nation of self-disciplined individuals, armed and ready to protect themselves and their property, can never be invaded successfully from without or within. In hundreds of years, Switzerland never has been. Furthermore, Finland was the only country to repel Russian military advances during World War II and as a result remained free. The reason for her success was the self-disciplined, well-trained, highly armed citizenry. They were unconquerable—as free, thinking people ought to and must be.

The gun control legislation being introduced in Congress is an insult to a free people. In fact, it puts them on notice that their freedom is in jeopardy. The warning bell is ringing. Americans owe their freedom and independence to well-armed citizens, willing to fight for what they believe in. Without arms, that freedom and independence, obtained at so high a price, cannot be retained. First we lost our gold money, now our guns, soon our property, then our liberty, finally our lives.

What are some of the informed people saying about this proposed legislation? Ferris E. Lucas, Executive Director of the National Sheriffs' Association, said, "If our guns are taken away from us, murders and robberies will increase. If law-abiding citizens had no guns for protection, and the only people with guns were the criminals, we would be helpless."[7] In full agreement is Los Angeles Chief of Police Edward Davis, who does not want gun controls because he believes that privately owned guns provide *personal and national defense.*

Modern sociologists and their kind would like to see guns outlawed; then their power-lust could reign supreme. First they disarm the mind in public schools, then disarm the body in reality. What a field-day there would be for the lowest elements of society. Where does justice fit in? It does not; it has been outlawed. The situation is one-sided, with all rights and privileges on the side of the criminal element. It is the epitome of injustice.

For proof, here are the answers given by eleven prisoners to some questions asked by California State Senator H.L. Richardson.[8] All had committed crimes with weapons.

1. Do handgun registration laws keep the criminal from using handguns in the commission of a crime? A. Two said yes; nine said, "No effect at all."

2. Do they deter criminals from getting handguns? A. Nine said, "Absolutely not, it had no impact whatsoever."

3. Does suspected gun ownership in a residence deter burglaries of that residence? A. Ten said yes; one said no.

4. Do you know of any specific case where a robbery was not performed because the occupant was known to be armed? A. Nine said yes.

5. When planning a robbery, does the criminal take into consideration the presence of weapons in deciding if the robbery will be attempted? A. All said yes.

6. Do businesses develop reputations for the use of handguns as defense against burglaries? A. 70% said yes. One prisoner volunteered, "We know of this place in Berkeley that used to be hit. Then the owner killed three guys. Nobody robs that place anymore."

7. If guns were totally banned, would you be able to get one? A. Unanimous yes.

8. Who benefits most from the registration of handguns, the criminal or the citizen? A. Most said the criminal. One prisoner was all for registration. He would love it; what a really grand idea.

The above is plain common sense. The criminals probably understand better than most because they are, to a great extent, public school drop-outs, still able to think.

The evil of gun control is a monstrous affront to the intelligence of a free man. It defies all consideration of justice. It proves there is no end to government's arrogant, diabolical, and tyrannical intentions.

The solutions to crime are a just society and punishments that fit the crime. Get tough on criminals, not victims, is what is needed. More crimes are committed because more criminals are walking the streets, not because law-abiding citizens are in possession of firearms which they are using in a responsible manner.

There is a sinister side to this legislation, too. Since guns are inanimate objects without wills or the ability to act on their own, there is really no need to control them. Therefore, gun control is, in essence, "people control." In addition, controls would deprive people of their most effective means of self-defense.

Outlawing guns creates another "victimless crime." This government prohibition amounts to an abrogation of the right to property. Why does not the government ban cars, knives, etc., too? Gun control is *immoral,* not because the Constitution guarantees the right to keep and bear arms, but by virtue of man's natural right to defend his own life. This becomes crucial when one realizes that the police cannot protect all the citizens since they are set up to apprehend a criminal after a crime has been committed, not to prevent the crime.

Another point is that gun laws have either no effect or an effect opposite to what the legislators wanted. For example, in 1966, eighty-seven percent of all gun crimes in New York City, where handguns are *totally* banned, were committed with unregistered weapons. In Detroit, in 1971, seventy-five percent of the shootings involved unregistered handguns. Consequently, when governments outlaw a commodity, a black market is set up to meet demand.

The Prohibition Era ought to have proven that. Drug traffic, which is accelerating, is another example of a black market moving in when the white market is outlawed. The net result is an increase in taxes, bureaucracues and the size of law enforcement agencies.

The campaign for gun control, however, avoids the real issue. In the end, individuals need guns to protect themselves not only from individual criminals, but from mass criminals—governments.

Robert Kulka, author of *Gun Control*, reports that the disarmament techniques of totalitarian states exhibit certain patterns. For instance, coincidental with the Nazi invasion of Czechoslovakia the arms registration lists of that country were seized by the Fifth Column and public disarmament thereby facilitated. Just before the Red puppet government assumed control of Hungary about 1948, all public and private shooting clubs were disbanded by police decree, and all private arms were taken into custody to "protect the people." Upon assuming power in Cuba, Castro utilized the gun registration instituted by Batista to confiscate privately owned guns. The Greek military junta, which overthrew that nation's democratic government in 1967, also launched an offensive against private ownership of guns.

People are not usually deprived of their liberties all at once, but gradually, by one encroachment after another; gun control is just another step in the eradication of our rights. And the victims, as usual, are sanctioning it. Patrick Henry believed that principles are too abstract for most people's comprehension. He said that if you tell them about the robbery of their property and that the next step will be to disarm them, "you bring the subject home to their bosoms, and they will be ready to fly to arms to defend themselves."

Well, now is the time to cry out—let your voice be heard! In the past ten years violent crimes are up 174 percent: murder is committed every 27 minutes, up 129 percent; rape every 10 minutes, up 192 percent; robbery every 82 seconds, up 226 percent, and the list goes on.[9] Rather than disarming the citizens, it might be a good idea to arm them to the teeth instead.

All liberty-loving people ought to want to see an armed and alert citizenry. Knowing how prone to rule our aspiring government on the Potomac is, we should all feel at ease knowing there are millions of guns in private hands in the United States.

There are car bumper stickers that sum up the situation: "When Guns Are Outlawed, Only Outlaws [including governments] Will Have Guns," which means, "When Only the Police Have Guns, the Police State Is Just Around the Corner." It is folly to relax one's vigilance against such obvious designs and pretensions. The handwriting is on the wall for all who will but read it.

What can be done? Besides demanding that gun control legislation be thrown out, make it obvious to your representatives that you are hereby serving notice that all laws intending to restrict the right of American citizens to keep and bear arms are unconstitutional; and all officials who violate their oaths of office by advocating and/or supporting such laws are, by definition, guilty of subverting, or attempting to subvert, the Constitution, the supreme law of the land.

No one in this nation has authority to disarm American citizens, as the Constitution forbids it, in whole and in part. The malfeasant official who presumes to try should be made summarily subject to fine, imprisonment, and forfeiture of office.

In 1830 when de Tocqueville visited the United States there were no internal police forces. Since then, the F.B.I., the C.I.A., and the I.R.S. have been created. And all sorts of crimes have proliferated. When America was free from internal police forces, she had little crime; de Tocqueville observed: "In America the means that the authorities have at their disposal for the discovery of crimes and the arrest of criminals are few. A state police does not exist, and passports are unknown....Yet I believe that in no country does crime more rarely elude punishment. The reason is that everyone conceives himself to be interested in furnishing evidence of the crime and in seizing the delinquent....In America he [the criminal] is looked upon as an enemy of the human race, and the whole of mankind is against him."[10]

In sum, Herbert Spencer wrote this prediction in July, 1898 to Grant Allen: "I said, just as you say, that we are in course of rebarbarisation, and that there is no prospect but that of military despotisms, which we are rapidly approaching."

NOTES ON GUN CONTROL, CHAPTER XVIII

1. *Conceived in Liberty*, Vol. 3, P. 201.
2. IBID., P. 318.
3. IBID., P. 320.
4. IBID.
5. *Annals of America*, Vol. 4, Pp. 72-3.
6. Bramble Minibooks, Box 836, Lansing, MI 48904, $1.
7. *Argosy Hunting Annual*, 1976, P. 72.
8. IBID., Pp. 72-73.
9. *One Nation Under God*, P. 272.
10. *Democracy in America*, Vol. I, P. 95.

XIX

Changing a Republic

The time to guard against corruption and tyranny is before they shall have gotten hold of us. It is better to keep the wolf out of the fold, than to trust to drawing his teeth and talons after he shall have entered.

THOMAS JEFFERSON

The purpose of this chapter is to show how far down the road of totalitarian government the United States has come. It begins with an article which lists some of the key steps necessary to change a free republic into a dictatorship. Then it discusses the infringements already committed on the Bill of Rights. Then finally, it shows how the United States has drifted closer to the principles of the *Communist Manifesto*, away from those of the U.S. Constitution.

Philip Freneau, an experienced journalist, edited the paper, the *National Gazette*. So effective a writer was Freneau that Jefferson credited him with saving the country when it was "galloping fast into monarchy." Below are excerpts from an editorial typical of those in which Freneau criticized Hamilton's economic programs from 1791 to 1793. It is entitled: "Rules for Changing a Limited Republican Government into an Unlimited Hereditary one;" it was dated July, 1792.

> [1.] It being necessary...to get rid of constitutional shackles and popular prejudices, all possible means and occasions are to be used....
>
> [2.] In drawing all bills, resolutions, and reports, keep constantly in view that the limitations in the Constitution are ultimately to be explained away. Precedents and phrases may thus be shuffled in,...of which good use may afterward be made.

[3.] Propagate the alien doctrines of monarchy and aristrocracy [or socialism]....
[4.] But the grand nostrum will be a public debt.... If by good fortune a debt be ready at hand, the most is to be made of it. Stretch it and swell it to the utmost the items will bear. Allow as many extra claims as decency will permit. Assume all the debts of your neighbors—in a word, get as much debt as can be raked and scraped together, and when you have got all you can, "advertise" for more, and have the debt made *as big as possible*. This object being accomplished, the next will be to make it *as perpetual as possible;* and the next to that, to get it into *as few hands as possible*. The more effectually to bring this about, modify the debt, complicate it, divide it, subdivide it, subtract it, postpone it... To be brief, let the whole be such a mystery that a *few only* can understand it; and let all possible opportunities and informations fall in the way of *these few* to clinch their advantages over the many.
[5.] The ways in which a great debt...will contribute to the ultimate end [is it] will require great taxes; great taxes, many taxgatherers and other officers; and all officers are auxiliaries of power. Heavy taxes may produce discontents; these may threaten resistance; and in proportion to this danger will be the pretense for a standing army to repel it....
[6.] The management of a great funded debt and an extensive system of taxes will afford a plea, not to be neglected, for establishing a great incorporated bank.... If the Constitution, according to its fair meaning, should not authorize it, so much the better. Push it through by a forced meaning and you will get in the bargain an admirable precedent for future misconstructions.

In fashioning the bank, remember that it is to be made particularly instrumental in enriching and aggrandizing the elect few....Money will be put under the direction of government, and government under the direction of money. To crown the whole, the bank will have a proper interest in swelling and perpetuating the public debt and public taxes, with all the blessings of both, because its agency and its profits will be extended in exact proportion.

> [7.] The expediency of seizing every occasion of external danger for augmenting and perpetuating the standing military force is too obvious to escape....
> [8.] The same prudence will improve the opportunity afforded by an increase of military expenditures for perpetuating the taxes required for them....
> [9.] Divide and govern....
> [10.] As it is not to be expected that the change of a republic into a monarchy [or socialist government]...can be carried through without occasional suspicions and alarms, it will be necessary to be prepared for such events. The best general rule on the subject is to be taken from the example of crying "Stop thief" first—neither lungs nor pens must be spared in charging every man who whispers, or even thinks, that the revolution on foot is meditated, with being himself an enemy to the established government and meaning to overturn it. Let the charge be reiterated and reverberated till at last such confusion and uncertainty be produced that the people, being not able to find out where the truth lies, withdraw their attention from the contest.
>
> Many other rules of great wisdom and efficacy might be added; but it is conceived that the above will be abundantly enough for the purpose. This will certainly be the case if the people can be either kept asleep so as not to discover, or be thrown into artificial divisions [polarized] so as not to resist, what is silently going forward...."[1]

The remainder of the chapter will illustrate the steps by which the American republic is being transformed into a foreign type of government, totally alien to our birthright of freedom. The following is a summary of how the Bill of Rights has been "explained away."

The First Amendment guarantees the rights to freedom of religion, speech, press, and assembly. Since the Income Tax Amendment has bought-off the church, there is no longer heard opposition to the usurpation of rights by government from the members of the church, as was heard during the Revolutionary era; there is little separation between state and church. Free speech is not entirely free since the radio and television airways are highly regulated, censored and licensed by the Federal Communications Commission. In addition, one can only assume the press is intimidated by government since it not only ignores covering anything in favor of individual rights (the growing tax rebellion), but fails to throw light on the usurpations of government activities (I.R.S. actions).

[1]*Annals of America,* Vol. 3, Pp. 499-504.

The Securities and Exchange Commission rules the investment field with an iron hand. If the news published by someone is not to its liking, it can and often does persecute that person by driving him out of business and even out of the country. "Whenever Truth is dangerous, Liberty is precarious," warned *Cato.*

The Second Amendment guarantees the right to keep and bear arms. This Amendment is under attack now by our "protector" government. With any foothold achieved, the confiscation of all arms is a dead certainty. What frightful plans does the government have in store for us that it must disarm us first?

The Third Amendment, no soldier should be quartered in any house in peacetime without the consent of the owner, is the *only* Amendment still respected.

The Fourth is the right to be secure in persons, houses, papers and effects against unreasonable search and seizure. The I.R.S. has usurped this right, for nothing is safe from its unlimited power.

Number Five guarantees no one shall be deprived of life, liberty, or property without due process of law; it also guarantees that no one shall be a witness against himself. The I.R.S. here, too, has usurped both rights. It is no wonder that nearly every American is intimidated and petrified of the inquisitorial I.R.S. It is the *essence* of evil.

The Sixth Amendment guarantees the right to a speedy and public trial and to be confronted with the witnesses against oneself. With the court system jammed as a result of "victimless crimes," there is no room for the real criminals. Hence, there is nothing speedy about today's justice system. Furthermore, the I.R.S. has ignored this right altogether. These infringements are a stain upon the reputation of every single honest American.

Amendment Seven guarantees a trial by jury. Many judges have denied this right in tax cases before the court.

Number Eight bars excessive fines and cruel and unusual punishment. Convicted murderers are sometimes set free on technicalities, while taxpayers, committing a "crime against the state," are incarcerated. In fact, the United States is the only country where tax evasion is a crime!

The Ninth Amendment guarantees all rights not enumerated in the Constitution. Also, no right enumerated can deny any others retained. This means that rights not heretobefore listed, such as running one's own business free of government rules, regulation, controls, and bureaucracies, are still guaranteed. But, of course, this is a sham, since the government has ridden roughshod over most individual rights.

The Tenth Amendment reserves *all* powers, not delegated to the federal government, to the states and/or the people. This Amendment is totally ignored. For examples, the federal government has created a central bank, made paper legal tender in payment of debts, instituted a progressive income tax, interfered in trade and commerce, conscripted citizens, supported a standing army, interfered in the business of foreign governments, and is surely working toward nationalizing the school system, to name but a few. *NONE* of these powers were delegated to the federal government by the Constitution.

Nine out of ten Amendments have been infringed upon or totally disregarded. This is outrageous! But where is the public outcry? As Jefferson said, "An elective despotism was not the government we fought for." Are we to have no rights left, except the right to obey?

But wait, there is more. Article 4, Section 4 of the Constitution guarantees a republican form of government. Originally, the Senate was elected by the state legislatures and the President was indirectly elected by the Electoral College. That has been changed. Starting with the Twelfth Amendment, the electors who originally voted for the two best men, the most popular becoming President, the second becoming Vice-President, now vote for the President and Vice-President together. This drastically lowers the chance of the two best qualified men becoming President and Vice President.

Then Amendment Seventeen changed the method of electing senators from the state legislatures to direct vote of the people. The Senate alone forecast the continued existence of the states. And before long it looks like the Electoral College will be abolished and replaced by the people directly electing the President (dictator). The plan to have changed the republic into a democracy will then be completed.

Amendment Fourteen, Section 4, says the validity of the public debt shall not be questioned. That would seem to legalize the national debt.

Amendments Fifteen and Twenty-Four usurp the states' rights to designate the qualifications of voters.

The famous Sixteenth Amendment perverts the justice of every person paying an equal tax to support government. Since no one knows how much his neighbor has paid, it is very easy for the federal government to grant huge sums of money to one group, state, or area at the expense of another. If all were taxed equally this form of bribery would be obvious.

Amendments Eighteen and Twenty-one *tested* the extent of the government's arbitrary power by first prohibiting and then repealing prohibition of the sale of intoxicating liquors.

Amendment Nineteen extended the vote to women, thereby broadening the democracy. The Twenty-sixth Amendment reduced the voting age from twenty-one years to eighteen. This extends the vote to every citizen over the age of eighteen regardless of qualifications.

Amendment Twenty-three gives the District of Columbia, the seat of government, their own electors to vote for President and Vice-President.

Amendment Twenty-five gives the President power to replace the Vice-President, superceding the customary rotation of office. The ease with which this has worked has been exhibited in the forced resignation of Vice-President Spiro Agnew, the appointment of Gerald Ford, the resignation of Richard Nixon, and the appointment of Nelson Rockefeller. Within a period of months, the elected officials had been replaced by nonelected, personally chosen, hand-picked men. No one said a word; no press questioned it. Out went the elected two and in went the selected two, all very legal. But, oh, so unrepublican and undemocratic!

The 1700 s were the years of the great republicans; they produced the Bill of Rights. The 1800 s ushered in the democrats with four amendments. The 1900 s have witnessed the busy-body socialists with eleven amendments, so far.

This change in government started when Henry asked, "Who authorized them (the framers) to speak the language of, *we the people,* instead of *we the States?*" It was a national government from the beginning, with the power to tax and to raise an army—the power over purse and sword.

Once a republic is changed into a democracy it will slide rapidly into totalitarianism. Although the chapter on socialism discussed the theoretical disadvantages of the system, it did not go into the ultimate aim of the socialist state, which is communism. That will be discussed here.

All communist countries practice socialism as their economic system. The plan they follow comes from the *Communist Manifesto,* authored by Karl Marx and Friedrich Engles. It is opposed to *all* individual rights; it sets up the government as sole owner of all life, liberty and property in the country. Here is what the *Manifesto*'s goals are:

1. Abolition of property in land and application of all rents of land to public purposes.
2. A heavy progressive or graduated income tax.
3. Abolition of all right of inheritance.
4. Confiscation of the property of all emigrants and rebels.
5. Centralization of credit in the hands of the state by means of a national bank with state capital and an exclusive monopoly.
6. Centralization of the means of communication and transport in the hands of the state.
7. Extension of factories and instruments of production owned by the state; the bringing into cultivation of waste lands, and the improvement of the soil generally in accordance with a common plan.
8. Equal obligation of all to work. Establishment of industrial armies, especially for agriculture.
9. Combination of agriculture with manufacturing industries;

gradual abolition of the distinction between town and country by a more equable distribution of the population over the country.

10. Free education for all children in public schools.

If this plan seems too remote to accept, please note that numbers 2, 5 and 10 are already in effect now. Numbers 3, 6 and 7 are being put into effect as fast as they can be made acceptable—especially number 3.

Number 9 is already on the books as Presidential Directive No. 11647. Its official name is Federal Regionalism Planning. The federal government is already expropriating the land of the states and its citizens. It is literally grabbing all the land possible to be put under government control. The United States has been divided into ten Federal Regional Councils, which will eventually abolish the states; under the guise of revenue-sharing it is regulating the sale and use of all the land in the country. The end result will be serfdom, i.e., slavery.

This threat cannot be overemphasized. In the April 16, 1973, Boston *Globe*, the former chairman of the Vermont House Appropriations Committee was quoted: "I advocate nothing less than doing away with private ownership as it concerns real estate." On July 24, 1974 he declared: "The property you possess in the form of real estate does not belong to you. It belongs to the government and the government is the people." (*Reason*, October, 1976.)

Many states are making progress in repelling this bureraucratic invasion, namely Indiana, Nevada, Illinois, South Dakota and others. The key to reversing this disastrous trend is state legislatures, because it is the power of the states that is being directly violated and usurped. For further information contact the Committee to Restore the Constitution, P.O. Box 986, Fort Collins, Colorado 80522.

With nearly seventy percent of the plan in force, how can one doubt the direction of current legislation. While the public sleeps, the plan "is silently going forward."

The *Manifesto* says "There are...eternal truths such as freedom, justice, etc., that are common to all states of society. But Communism abolishes eternal truths, it abolishes all religion and all morality,...it, therefore, acts in contradiction to all past historical experience." In short, communism admits it contradicts the essence of human nature. Nevertheless, it is human nature that they insist must change. And they are prepared to sacrifice humanity for their irrational goal.

In the *Manifesto's* own words, it plans to abolish the family unit, countries and nationalities, private property, and the individual: "...that by 'individual' you mean...the middle class owner of property. This person must, indeed, be swept out of the way and made impossible." By middle class it means exactly that, the huge American middle class, i.e., you, dear reader, who own (or are paying on) your house, car, furniture, and other necessities and/or luxuries. This is the essence of socialism—the eradication of the individual and all he possesses—his family, his rights, and his property. No greater injustice has ever been or ever will be perpetrated on mankind.

The time in which to reverse this trend is growing short. There is talk of replacing our "out-dated" Constitution with a new one. But judging from the prevalent philosophy of today's culture and its "intellectuals," that can only spell disaster. The time to act is NOW, while the Constitution is still in force, while the majority of Americans have no desire to be herded like cattle into a master plan under the guise of being "taken care of."

It is illuminating that Marx did not think a violent revolution would be necessary in the United States to bring about communism. He figured that since it is a democracy, the citizens would eventually vote themselves into socialism first, then communism. He has been right so far.

To fight socialism one must remember that our rights are created in us by the laws of nature. They are born with us, exist with us; and cannot be taken from us by any human power without taking our lives. In short, they are founded on the immutable maxims of reason and justice. One cannot fight against an idea, i.e., socialism or communism, per se. One must fight for something, i.e., individual rights and free enterprise.

Justice demands that free people shoulder the responsibility, accept the risks and receive the rewards, if any, of being free men. A paternal government is a tyrannical government—what it gives it can take away. It takes a free man to remain free; a slave never regains his freedom.

According to Hamilton in *The Federalist*, No. 33, "If the federal government should overpass the just bounds of its authority and make a tyrannical use of its powers, the people, whose creature it is, must appeal to the standard they have formed, and take such measures to redress the injury done to the Constitution as the exigency may suggest and prudence justify."

"The secret of freedom," observed Pericles, "is courage".

XX

How to Return to Justice

If ye love wealth better than liberty, the tranquility of servitude better than the animating contest of freedom, go home from us in peace. We ask not your counsels or arms. Crouch down and lick the hands which feed you. May your chains set lightly upon you, and may posterity forget that ye were our countrymen.
SAMUEL ADAMS, 1776

It has been shown throughout the book that justice in the political sphere is the very basis of a good society. And a government which respects individual rights and private property will *not* interfere in its citizens' personal lives nor in economics—the marketplace. In contrast, a government seeking to enslave its people will continually interfere in their lives, liberties and property, under one pretext or another. Thus it follows that politicians hold the power of life or death over their constituents. One can only ignore politics and politicians at one's peril.

Today there is a dichotomy between the rights to liberty and property. It is this dichotomy which is splitting the country apart and keeping us at cross-purposes. One faction, for example, defends civil liberties (condemning wars, supporting the right to drugs, gambling, etc.), *but* it condemns the individual's right to the fruits of his labor by favoring progressive taxation and confiscatory inheritance taxes. On the other hand, the other faction defends all forms of property and wealth ownership *except* that of the person. It favors low taxation and is opposed to inheritance taxes, *but* opposes civil liberties by defending government interference into and prohibition of drugs, gambling, etc. and any other form of personal conduct that offends its sense of morals. It also supports involvement in foreign wars and conscription. This is what civil wars are made of.

Government, of course, has made the most of this dichotomy by expanding its power base. It has avoided acting to protect individual rights. It gets involved in foreign wars, conscripts free men, regulates individual conduct, taxes all forms of property and income, and confiscates inheritances. Its method is a classical illustration of divide and conquer or control. Social power is diminishing while government power is increasing.

What this country needs now is a united, consistent philosophy, based on justice, with no dichotomy between liberty and property. Since principles never change, honest men should be able to agree on a just political system, a fair and equitable system that guarantees all rights to all citizens for all times, where there is no dichotomy between liberty and property—which are the cornerstones of a free society.

That was Jefferson's philosophy. He also believed that free people ought to get very active politically, occasionally: "What country can preserve its liberties if its rulers are not warned from time to time, that the people preserve the spirit of resistance?" After all, people throwing off tyranny and oppression are not traitors. They are patriots. Old King George III's traitors are our beloved patriots. Therefore, the time has come for individual political action, to re-establish justice by re-establishing respect for individual liberty and property.

Americans are being kept so busy working to "make ends meet," that they have not had the time to get politically involved. Little do they realize that that is part of the conspiracy—keep the people so busy they cannot see what is going forward. Issues like gay rights, the Equal Rights Amendment, Panama Canal, Watergate, scandals, etc. are merely diversionary tactics. The real objectives such as regulations, victimless crimes, regionalism, not to mention the frightful possibility of a new Constitution, are in progress and pushing onward. But life is neither a joyride nor a burden; it is a serious job imposed on us, to be seen through to the end to our credit.

The alternative to correcting the injustices that exist in society today by way of a peaceful revolution in the ballot box is a violent rebellion in the streets. For that is the ultimate result of injustices and sufferings. Some suggestions have been offered to the reader throughout the course of the book. However, here they are summarized; they are the key issues of paramount importance. Here is how to have a successful revolution, how to return to justice:

1. Become active in local politics: property taxes, school bond levies, local and state budgets, etc.; use the letters-to-the-editor column in your local paper to further your ideas, question political action, make suggestions, etc.

2. Join and actively support these political action groups: Committee to Re-establish the Gold Standard (85 Fourth Avenue #6M, New York 10003, $10); Committee to Restore the Constitution (Box 986, Ft. Collins, Colorado 80522); National Rifle Association (1600 Rhode Island Avenue, Washington, D.C. 20036, $15).

3. Be informed; subscribe to and read these publications: *Spotlight* (300 Independence Avenue S.E., Washington, D.C. 20003, $16);

Liberty Lobby (same as *Spotlight*); *The Gold Bug* (same as CRGS); the *American Rifleman* (same as NRA).

4. Get to know your congressman personally, visit him when he is in town, take a committee along; write to him to give him your views, opinions, ideas, criticisms; he must come home for re-election every two years; he will listen to you. Also advise him of his Constitutional oath, if necessary.

In sum, work for repeal of the Sixteenth Amendment, the Internal Revenue Service, the Federal Reserve System, legal tender laws, future conscription plans. Work to support the re-establishment of the Gold Standard and all civil liberties and to protect the Second Amendment, the right to keep and bear arms; *all* gun control legislation should be terminated immediately and permanently.

The amount of government power will always increase to the level of the people's toleration. An extremely tolerant populace, for instance, will suffer a dictatorship. A moderately tolerant public will condone a democracy. An intolerant society will be free. It is time we became intolerant of government abuses and usurpations. As Paine said, "The man that does not now feel for the honor of the best and noblest cause that ever a country engaged in, and exert himself accordingly, is no longer worthy of a peaceable residence among a people determined to be free."

Furthermore, one is bound to throw off any form of tyranny because not to do so would be tacitly promoting slavery and misery and injustice. In this case, if you are not part of the solution, you are part of the problem. Evil exists because it goes unopposed. It but needs to be recognized for what it is and it will disappear.

Modern government is a protection racket. It cannot do its work without your consent, and if you do not withhold your consent you deserve it. If Americans should now turn back, submit again to slavery, it would be a betrayal so base the human race might better perish, and it might. Now that you know the truth about the country, stop supporting your own destroyers. The evil of the country is made possible by nothing but the sanction you give. Withdraw your sanction; withdraw your support.

The cause of freedom is a constant struggle requiring eternal vigilance and courage. Once obtained, freedom must be closely guarded. Churchill observed that everyone at some time must take up the gauntlet of liberty, and the sooner, the better: "If you will not fight for right when you can easily win without bloodshed; if you will not fight when your victory will be sure and not too costly; you may come to the moment when you will have to fight with all the odds against you and only precarious chance of survival.

"There may be even a worse case. You may have to fight when there is no hope of victory, because it is better to perish than live as slaves."

Bibliography

Acton, Lord, *Essays on Freedom and Power*, Cleveland, Ohio: The World Publishing Co., 1972, by arrangement with The Macmillan Co.

Aldridge, Alfred Owen, *Man Of Reason: The Life of Thomas Paine*, New York: J.B. Lippincott Co., 1959.

—*Benjamin Franklin: Philosopher and Man*, New York: J.B. Lippincott Co., 1965.

Annals of America, Chicago: Encyclopedia Britannica, Inc., 1968, Vol. 2, "Samuel Adams: The Rights of the Colonists."

—"Noah Webster: The Union of the American States."

—Vol. 3, "Noah Webster: Diseases of the Body Politic."

—"Richard Henry Lee: On the Rights that Must Be Preserved in the New Constitution."

—"Luther Martin: The People Versus The States."

—"Reasons for Dissent by the Anti-Federalists of Pennsylvania."

—"Debates in the Virginia Ratifying Convention."

—"Controversy Over the Constitutionality of a United States Bank."

—"James Madison: The Right to Property and Property in Rights."

—"Philip Freneau: Rules for Changing a Republic into a Monarchy."

—Vol. 4, "Opposition to a Standing Army."

—"Thomas Jefferson: A Simple and Inexpensive Government."

—"Thomas Jefferson: First Inaugural Address."

—"Albert Gallatin: The State of Manufacturing."

—"Thomas Jefferson: On Republican Government."

—"Thomas Jefferson: On Civil and Natural Rights."

—"Thomas Jefferson: The Roots of Democracy."

—"Anonymous: Opposition to Paper Money."

A Treasury of the World's Great Speeches, Selected and edited by Houston Peterson, New York: Grolier, Inc., 1973.

Bailyn, Bernard, *The Ideological Origins of the American Revolution*, Cambridge, Massachusetts: The Belknap Press of Harvard University Press, 1967.

—*The Origins of American Politics*, New York: Vintage Books, Division of Random House, 1970.

Bastiat, Frederic, *The Law*, Irvington-on-Hudson, New York: The Foundation for Economic Education, Inc., 1974.

Campion, Nardi Reeder, *Patrick Henry: Firebrand of the Revolution*, Boston: Little, Brown & Co., 1961.

Chodorov, Frank, *The Income Tax: The Root of All Evil*, Old Greenwich, Connecticut: The Devin-Adair Co., 1974.

Cooley, Marvin L., *The Big Bluff—Tax Tyranny in the Guise of Law,* Mesa, Arizona, 1972.

Donovan, Frank, *The Thomas Jefferson Papers*, New York: Dodd, Mead & Co., 1963.

Basic Writings of Thomas Jefferson, Edited by Philip S. Foner, Ph.D, Garden City, New York: Halcyon House, 1950, by special arrangement with Willey Book Co., 1944.

Johnson, Wallace, *A Fresh Look at Patriotism*, Old Greenwich, Conn: The Devin-Adair Co., 1976.

Great Books of the Western World, Robert Maynard Hutchins, Editor in Chief, Chicago: Encyclopedia Britannica, Inc., 1971. Volumes 3, 7, 9, 12, 14, 18, 23, 25, 35, 36, 38, 39, 43, 44.

Hayek, Friedrich A., *The Constitution of Liberty*, Chicago: A Gateway Edition, Henry Regnery Co., 1972.

—*The Road to Serfdom*, Chicago: The University of Chicago Press, 1969.

Henry, William Wirt, *Patrick Henry,* New York: Charles Scribner's Son's, 1891, Volumes I, II, III.

Hirst, Francis W., *Life and Letters of Thomas Jefferson,* New York: The Macmillan Co., 1926.

Katz, Howard S., *The Paper Aristocracy,* New York: Books in Focus, 1976.

Knollenberg, Bernhard, *Growth of the American Revolution 1766-1775,* New York: The Free Press, 1975.

Kotler, Milton, *Neighborhood Government: The Local Foundations of Political Life*, New York: The Bobbs-Merrill Co., Inc., 1969.

Kristol, Irving, *The American Revolution As A Successful Revolution,* Washington, D.C.: American Enterprise Institute for Public Policy Research, 1973, speech delivered at St. John's Church, Washington, D.C., October 12, 1973.

Lambro, Donald, *The Federal Rathole*, New Rochelle, New York: Arlington House, 1975.

Larson, Martin A., *Tax Revolt: U.S.A.! Why and How Thousands of Patriotic Americans Refuse to Pay the Income Tax,* Washington, D.C.: Liberty Lobby, 1973.

Leon, Sy, *None of the Above: The Lesser of Two Evils... Is Evil*, Santa Ana, California: Fabian Publishing Co., 1976.

Libertarian Directories:

—*In Pursuit of Liberty,* Phoenix, Arizona: RB Press.

—*The Freedom Fighter Index,* L.T. Patterson Strategy, Box 37432, Cincinnati, Ohio 45237.

Main, Jackson Turner, *The Anti-Federalists: Critics of the Constitution 1781-1788*, New York: W.W. Norton and Co., Inc., 1961.

Malone, Dumas, *Jefferson and His Time*, Volume 1: *Jefferson the Virginian*, Boston: Little, Brown & Co., 1948.

—Volume 2: *Jefferson and the Rights of Man*, 1951.

The Vintage Mencken, Gathered by Alistair Cooke, New York: Vintage Books, various dates.

Morse, John T. Jr., *American Statesman: Benjamin Franklin*, Boston: Houghton, Mifflin & Co., 1889.

Nock, Albert Jay, *Jefferson*, New York: Harcourt, Brace & Co., 1926.

—*Our Enemy, The State*, New York: Free Life Editions, 1973.

—*The Memoirs of a SuperfluousMan*, Chicago: Henry Regnery Co., A Gateway Edition, 1969.

Paterson, Isabel, *The God of the Machine*, Caldwell, Idaho: The Caxton Printers, Ltd., 1968.

Peterson, Merrill D., *Thomas Jefferson and the New Nation*, New York: Oxford University Press, 1970.

Rand, Ayn, *Capitalism: The Unknown Ideal*, New York: The New American library, various dates.

—*Atlas Shrugged,* New York: Random House, 1957.

Rothbard, Murray N., *Conceived in Liberty*, New Rochelle, New York: Arlington House, Volumes I and II, 1975, Volume III, 1976.

Sidney, Algernon, *Discourses Concerning Government*, England: Gregg International Publishers, Ltd., 1968, 3rd Edition, MDCCLI, Republished.

Spencer, Herbert, *The Man Versus The State*, Introduction by Albert Jay Nock, Caldwell, Idaho: The Caxton Printers, Ltd., 1969.

Tocqueville, Alexis de, *Democracy in America*, The Henry Reeve Text, Volume I, New York: Alfred A. Knopf, 1945.

—*Democracy in America*, Volume II.

—*Journey to America*, Translated by George Lawrence, Edited by J.P. Mayer, New Haven, Connecticut: Yale University Press, 1960.

—*Recollections,* Translated by G. Lawrence, Edited by J.P. Mayer and A.P. Kerr, Garden City, New York: Doubleday & Co., Inc., 1970.

Trenchard, John and Gordon, Thomas, *Cato's Letters: Essays on Liberty, Civil and Religious, and Other Important Subjects*, New York: Da Capo Press, 1971, Volume I & II.

Tyler Moses Coit, *American Statesman: Patrick Henry*, Largepaper edition, edited by John T. Morse, Jr., New York: Houghton, Mifflin & Co., 1898.

Van der Weyde, William M., *The Life and Works of Thomas Paine*, Patriot's Edition, Introduction by Thomas A. Edison, New Rochelle, New York: Thomas Paine National Historical Association, 1925, Volumes I-VI.

Walton, Rus, *One Nation Under God*, Old Tappan, New Jersey: Fleming H. Revell Co., 1975.

Wells, Alden Rice, *The New Monroe Doctrine, Role of the Navy,* Lansing, Michigan: Bramble Minibooks.

Willison, George F., *Patrick Henry and His World*, Garden City, New York: Doubleday & Co., Inc., 1969.

YOUR TAXES ARE GOING UP; YOUR ELECTRIC AND GAS BILLS ARE COSTING MORE; AND THE GOVERNMENT IS TELLING YOU TO USE YOUR AIR CONDITIONER LESS IN THE SUMMER—WHY?

FOR AN ENERGY CRISIS THAT DOESN'T EXIST

In ENERGY: THE CREATED CRISIS, Antony C. Sutton confirms the suspicion long held by many Americans that the energy "crisis" is a hoax perpetrated on the American people by big government aided and abetted by big business.

Inside are the details on:

- *America's present energy reserves—enough for the next 2000 years*
- *How and why the U.S. government works to obstruct energy development*
- *Which huge multi-national oil companies are most politically active in supporting the government's efforts to encourage the energy "crisis"—and why*
- *Nuclear energy—far cheaper and safer than oil, coal and gas*
- *The Carter energy plan—a taxation plan in disguise*
- *The ruling elite—who they are and how they're working against you*

To order, send **$10.95** (plus **80¢** p. & h.) to: BOOKS IN FOCUS. 30 day return privilege.

POWER IS OURS

Buthelezi Speaks on the Crisis in South Africa

"The speeches of *BUTHELEZI* provide a tremendous source of material . . . on the South African Problem . . . The reader will gain new insight as he is led by this gifted mind and articulate person . . . It's extremely important that (he) is heard and understood . . . he has earned the right to be heard."

Rev. Leon H. Sullivan
Director, General Motors Corporation
Minister, Zion Baptist Church
Author of the Sullivan Code of Ethics for American Companies operating in South Africa

An epic struggle is unfolding in South Africa—a struggle destined to affect the entire world. At the forefront of this movement a leader has arisen.

A *MAN* whose existence cannot be ignored by the South African or world media;

A *MAN* too powerful to be dealt with in typical Apartheid fashion;

A *MAN* who combines rare qualities of leadership, intellect, organization, and courage;

A *MAN* whose hour has come.

This man is Gatsha Buthelezi. He is the leader of 5,000,000 Zulu people in South Africa; he is the Chairman of INKATHA and of the South African Black Alliance.

This book contains some of his most powerful speeches, covering every topic of importance in the South African dilemma. As you read through its pages you will be drawn into Gatsha's struggle and life, and will share his moment in history.

Topics are indexed by a unique "Idea Index."

To order send $12.95 (plus 80¢ p.&h.) to Books In Focus. 30 day return privilege.

Immortal Light of Genius

Flight

In this volume
you will find the immortal light
of genius at its moments of greatest
inspiration discovering truth, creating
beauty, moving Humanity to fulfill its
dream of Glory. . . freedom, achievement
and joy.

Touch this blue fire of genius, this
immortal light, this glory, with your
mind and with your heart and it will
set fire to your spirit.

The immortal light of genius
is the energy for life.

To order send $5.95 (plus 80¢ p.&h.) to Books In Focus. 30 day return privilege.

BARNARD
SOUTH AFRICA: SHARP DISSECTION

Christiaan Barnard, the world renowned South African heart surgeon speaks his mind on the dilemma in his country, and other trouble spots in Africa.

"In an unquestionably heartfelt expression of his views as a white Afrikaner proud of his heritage and land, he asserts his reasoned opinion that apartheid should be ended immediately — for practical as well as moral reasons."—PUBLISHERS WEEKLY (review)

Here is a view of South Africa for the reader who wants to form his own judgment, a view based on practical knowledge of the situation as analyzed by an intelligent mind. As the situation there threatens to explode and intrude more and more into our lives, concerned persons will want to understand this viewpoint.

To order, send $8.80, hardback (includes postage) to Books In Focus. 30 day return privilege.